Dr Mark Pearson is a journalist, author and professor of journalism at Bond University. He holds a PhD examining Internet journalism and a Master of Laws with a focus on media law. Professor Pearson is a correspondent for Reporters Without Borders and has been published in the *Wall Street Journal*, the *Far Eastern Economic Review* and *The Australian* newspapers.

Blog: journlaw.com | Twitter: @journlaw | Facebook: Journ Law.

Also by Mark Pearson
The Journalist's Guide to Media Law (with Mark Polden)
Breaking into Journalism (with Jane Johnston)

MARK PEARSON

BLOGGING &TWEETING WITHOUT GETTING SUED

A GLOBAL GUIDE TO THE LAW FOR ANYONE WRITING ONLINE

ALLEN&UNWIN

First published in 2012

Copyright © Mark Pearson 2012

Allen & Unwin
Sydney, Melbourne, Auckland, London
83 Alexander Street
Crows Nest NSW 2065
Australia

Phone: (61 2) 8425 0100
Fax: (61 2) 9906 2218
Email: info@allenandunwin.com
Web: www.allenandunwin.com

Cataloguing-in-Publication details are available from the National Library of Australia

www.trove.nla.gov.au

ISBN 978 1 74237 877 0

Set in 10.9/14 pt Fairfield LT Std by Bookhouse, Sydney
Printed and bound in Australia by SOS Print + Media Group

10 9 8 7 6

For our brand-new grandchild—
Beatrice Elizabeth Staughton

CONTENTS

Preface   ix

Introduction   xiii

Chapter 1   Down to basics: the legal risks of going global
             in a flash   1

Chapter 2   Cyberlibel and reputational damage online   19

Chapter 3   See you in court . . .   45

Chapter 4   Identity, anonymity and deception   63

Chapter 5   Privacy and security   86

Chapter 6   Confidentiality in a medium with few secrets   107

Chapter 7   The fine line between opinion and bigotry   125

Chapter 8   Copycats and corporate capers   145

Chapter 9   Big Brother and you: censorship hotspots and
             security laws   166

Resources   Read all about it!   184

Notes   194

PREFACE

The roots of this book can be traced back more than thirty years to when I was a cub reporter for a suburban newspaper. After only a few weeks in the job I wrote a story about a disgruntled patient who was complaining about the negligence of the local hospital. A few days later I was summoned to my manager's office and was told the hospital was suing for defamation. The newspaper negotiated a $10,000 settlement. My editor let me keep my job. 'But you'd better learn something about the law,' he advised. I've devoted much of the past three decades to doing just that and the process has continued in this project.

This book is for the countless bloggers and social media users who realise they now have the same legal obligations as large media organisations, but lack their experience, knowledge and muscle. We are all international publishers now—every time we blog, tweet or comment on a website—and are subject to the laws of several hundred legal jurisdictions worldwide.

There is no way a small book like this can cover the laws of all of those nations, states, provinces and territories. For that reason, most of the examples and discussion focus on the English-speaking world: the US, the UK, Canada, Australia and other Commonwealth countries. But you'll also find many examples from Europe and other parts of the world.

My aims are modest: to introduce you to some common legal principles that broadly apply to online publishing in many parts of the world and to bring them to life with the stories of bloggers and social media users who have encountered them. Some have defended their cases successfully while many others have been fined or jailed because of their ignorance or outright defiance of the law. Some have discovered their publications have broken the law in another nation when they would have been perfectly safe publishing the material at home.

This book can't give you specific legal advice, but hopefully you'll learn enough about basic blogging and social media law to avoid some of the main hazards and know when to seek the professional guidance of a lawyer.

And I must confess a bias. As a journalist, academic and blogger, I am a strong advocate for responsible free expression. My frank view is that there are far too many restrictions on that freedom in most parts of the world. If you can't change those laws at least you can try to understand them and navigate them effectively. Knowledge is power, and I hope this book helps empower your blogging.

•

There are too many friends, students, colleagues and tweeps to name here, but I must express special gratitude to the following:

- my wife, Julie, and family for their support through the process
- students Annabelle Cottee and Christian Huebenthal for their research assistance
- Bond University for allowing me the research time for the project
- Allen & Unwin publisher Elizabeth Weiss and senior editor Elizabeth Cowell for their sage advice, and editor Sarah Hazelton for her expert excisions and stylistic corrections
- faculty colleagues, my Twitter tweeps and Facebook friends who have generously provided many of the links to international examples in the book
- the students and journalists whose questions have helped direct my enquiries and fire my enthusiasm.

And, of course, my thanks go to you, dear reader, for buying this book or ebook and for investing your time in reading it. Please tweet me your reviews or suggestions for the next edition to @journlaw or post a comment on my blog at journlaw.com.

INTRODUCTION

Twitbrief: Blogging, Twitter, Facebook and the law: identifying and managing legal risks as a Web 2.0 publisher

Chicago interior designer Jill Maremont had established quite a following on her professional blog and on her Twitter and Facebook accounts. But in mid-September 2009 her life changed dramatically. She was crossing the street on an errand for her employer when a car ran a red light, smashed into a taxi, and then hit both Jill and a co-worker. As she was recovering in hospital from serious injuries she discovered her boss and another colleague were continuing to post and tweet under her name. The postings continued even after she objected. She sued over her rights to publicity and privacy.[1]

When former Assistant US Attorney Tad DiBiase posted a *Denver Post* article to his criminal law blog, nobodymurdercases.com, in 2010, he had no idea he would become the centre of landmark copyright dispute. With the backing of the Electronic Frontier Foundation,

DiBiase challenged the standing of a 'copyright troll' company, Righthaven, which had launched hundreds of similar actions over material from the *Denver Post* and the *Las Vegas Review-Journal*. Its business model was to hit small-time publishers with exorbitant copyright royalty claims and legal costs.

While DiBiase was fighting and winning his action,[2] on the other side of the globe Australian journalism academic Julie Posetti faced defamation action from a national daily newspaper editor who threatened to sue her over her tweets from an education conference. Posetti was reporting the proceedings to her several thousand followers and had quoted a reporter from the newspaper criticising her former boss during a speech. The editor claimed Posetti's tweets were inaccurate. She argued that they summarised the speaker's comments reasonably within Twitter's 140-character limit. The case raised questions about the suitability of Twitter for live reporting of events and about whether newspaper editors should resort to lawsuits.[3]

In the UK, some rash comments on a Facebook page were the recipe for £10,000 in defamation damages awarded against an English chef who had fallen out with a law student friend over a small debt. He posted an offensive image of a child along with the comment: 'Ray, you like kids and you are gay so I bet you love this picture, Ha ha'. That was enough for 24-year-old Jeremiah Barber to earn a conviction for publishing child pornography and to lose the libel suit.[4]

And then there is Cu Huy Ha Vu, who languishes in a Vietnamese jail after posting comments on his blog supporting a new system of government and granting interviews on the websites of Voice of America and Radio Free Asia. Vu joined at least sixteen other writers imprisoned in Vietnam for expressing their views online.

▶ Let's think globally

This book takes up the stories of scores of people like these to illustrate the main legal dangers facing bloggers and social media users in this exciting Web 2.0 global publishing environment.

Most books written about digital media law are hefty legal tomes focused on just one jurisdiction (legal system)—typically the US. This book is different in two key ways: it tries to break through the legal jargon to make the concepts understandable to the average blogger, and it recognises that, as an online writer, you need to know something about the media laws of other countries if that's where your work is being downloaded. It helps you learn from the experiences of other bloggers throughout the world who have been intimidated, sued, arrested and jailed. If you're lucky, it might even help you avoid those kinds of situations yourself.

Each time you post your latest blog update or social media message you may be subject to the laws of more than 600 nations, provinces, states and territories. Of course, you might not have 600 hits, views or retweets, so you might only be reaching some of them. But you can never quite be sure where your words, sounds and images might finish up.

▶ Legally, we're all 'publishers'

Like it or not, whether you have millions of followers for your tweets about 'shit your dad says' or just a single-figure readership for your blog on fifteenth-century tapestries, in the eyes of the law you are now a 'publisher'. That means you have to comply with those same communication laws that traditional publishers have been forced to obey since Gutenberg invented the printing press half a millennium ago. The big difference is that for most of that time publishers only had to worry about the laws in their own country. You have 600-plus legal systems or 'jurisdictions' to consider.

Your blog or microblog offers you potential access to a larger audience than even that enjoyed by the great publishers of the twentieth century—Lord Northcliffe in England, William Randolph Hearst in the US, and Rupert Murdoch, who established the global media conglomerate News Corporation. These media barons had teams of lawyers at their disposal to advise them on the risks they faced as their giant presses rolled each day. And they had war chests full of cash to stave off an action or appeal it to the highest courts. You might not be as big a target, but as a blogger or social media user you face considerable risks because of the international nature of your publications. But if you're an independent writer like me, you're pretty much on your own. Most of us do not have that scale of support when we find ourselves in the midst of a legal dispute we could never have anticipated. We may not have the wealth to defend a lawsuit or even to raise bail if we are charged with a publishing crime.

▶ Internet freedom with responsibility

Lawyers talk in terms of 'rights' and 'duties'. These are the yin and the yang of any legal situation. Every time you sit at the keyboard to draft a blog post or a tweet you exercise your right to free expression, but you have a legal duty not to trample on other people's rights in the process. Even in North America and Scandinavia, where free speech has strong constitutional protection, the courts still weigh your 'right to write' against the rights of other citizens—such as their rights to a fair trial, privacy, safety and good reputation.

As a blogger or social media user, whenever you press that Send or Publish button, most countries expect you to refrain from committing a crime, destroying someone's reputation, interfering with justice, insulting minorities, endangering national security or stealing other people's words and images.

Of course the most controversial example of bold Internet publishing has been the release of footage and classified documents by the WikiLeaks organisation since its 2006 launch. Its uploads of classified US diplomatic cables prompted several legal actions and threats, including the arrest and charging of an alleged source of the leaks, a court order that Twitter release information about member accounts, and threats of libel suits from both sides. But you would have to agree WikiLeaks went into the document dump with its eyes open—briefed by counsel from some of the world's leading news groups.

This book points out many of the legal risks you are taking as an online writer and gives you an idea of how those dangers vary in different parts of the world. The sad reality is that if you wanted to reduce your legal risk to zero you might never post anything online at all. The very act of publishing exposes you to a range of legal traps covered in this book: defamation, contempt of court, privacy breaches, identity theft, confidentiality, court orders, hate speech, state secrets, breach of copyright, false advertising and sedition.

Not even the courts know how to handle the huge changes triggered by the Internet and social media. When a judge issued a ban on the identification of an English footballer involved in an affair with another celebrity in 2011, more than 30,000 Twitter users faced jail for tweeting his name.[5]

Nothing will replace the need for sound legal advice if you are thinking of pushing the boundaries of media law in the online environment, but by the end of this book you should at least have a reasonable grasp of the basic legal challenges facing you as an author in this complex new world of cyber-publishing. Just hold off pressing that Send button on anything too controversial until you've finished reading it.

IN BRIEF: PUBLISHING ONLINE

- Your work is subject to laws wherever it is downloaded. That means you could be dealing with more than 600 different legal systems.

- In legal terms you are a 'publisher' whenever you post something. This means you are subject to the same laws as the big media businesses. But you probably don't have their expertise or resources.

- If in doubt, invest in some legal advice. You can't put a price on your liberty.

CHAPTER 1

DOWN TO BASICS: THE LEGAL RISKS OF GOING GLOBAL IN A FLASH

Twitbrief: Ups and downs of instant worldwide publication. #impulsiveness #liability #jurisdictions #FirstAmendment #publicinterest #malice

When sixteen-year-old Texan teenager Alison Chang flashed a 'V' sign in a travel snap taken by her church youth counsellor, she would never have imagined her image would be posted on a bus stop on the other side of the world,[1] triggering an international legal dispute over privacy, libel, contract, negligence, copyright and jurisdiction.

The multinational conglomerate Virgin Mobile had lifted the picture from the photo-sharing site Flickr as part of a billboard advertising campaign in Australia. It had plastered the slogan 'Dump your pen friend' above Alison's head and had put the caption 'Free text virgin to virgin' right under her image.

Alison's mother, Susan, sued on her behalf, along with the photographer, Justin Ho-Wee Wong, on a range of grounds in the US District Court in Texas. Mrs Chang claimed her daughter had been distressed after friends told her about the image, and said the captions had embarrassed the family in their church community. She said Alison had suffered 'humiliation, severe embarrassment, frustration, grief, and general mental anguish' through the misuse of her likeness.

Alison certainly seemed surprised when she was alerted to the Virgin campaign in a Flickr forum. Writing under the pen-name 'Aleeviation', she posted: 'hey that's me! no joke. i think i'm being insulted . . . can you tell me where this was taken?'

But after a two-year legal battle and considerable media attention, the court held it had no power to rule on the matter because the Singapore-based Virgin Mobile did not have enough of a connection with the state of Texas.

▶ **Ancient laws for a digital era**

There are many wonders of the Internet and social media we already take for granted. Just a few years ago a newspaper or magazine publisher would have to spend millions on printing presses and transport to reach an audience in just one city, and a reader would have to write a letter to respond to a story. Now, for next to nothing, we can reach a global audience on a hand-held device and start a conversation within seconds.

Our words and images transcend the world's borders and time zones and allow us to develop professional and personal relationships we could never have imagined last century. Magically, our creations are at once published instantly and archived forever. The downside is that these twenty-first-century digital marvels are mostly being regulated by the laws of a bygone era designed for traditional methods of publication: when newspapers were published in a single place, by a named person at a predictable time and the next day were used to wrap up the trash.

The decision in the Virgin Mobile case was bad news for Alison Chang's mother and the church photographer and might appear encouraging if you are worried about your legal liability in other places. But there have been several recent court decisions running counter to this one, so don't think you can post whatever you like from the sanctuary of your own country without any fear of legal consequences elsewhere.

Sometimes the same posting can trigger separate legal actions in different places. Courts and prosecutors might be at odds over whether the laws of one state or another apply to your online publication or social media posting. This legal area is known as 'conflict of laws'—and it is a specialised field of expertise. Sadly, legislators and judges throughout the world—with their nineteenth- and twentieth-century rituals and precedents—are way behind the pace of technological change and are finding it hard to adapt to the cross-border issues caused by Web 2.0. That's why we are getting differing decisions.

Some judges have tried to inject some predictability into their assessment of your liability from afar. A landmark case centred on a dispute between two companies over the use of the name 'Zippo'. One was a manufacturing company and the other an Internet news service provider. A Pennsylvania court developed a sliding scale to help it decide whether the web news service had enough commercial dealings in that state for the court to have jurisdiction.[2] Lawyers will usually need to show some level of connection between you and the place of the legal action against you before a court can hear the matter. If you are selling your services in that jurisdiction, if you are blogging for a larger organisation trading there, or if you happen to be visiting there, it might amount to enough of a connection to make you answerable to the laws of that place.

▶ You're published where your material is viewed

The High Court of Australia became the world's first senior judicial body to rule on the time and place of web publication in a trans-Pacific dispute in 2002. In *Dow Jones v Gutnick*,[3] judges had to decide whether Australian businessman Joseph Gutnick could sue US-based publisher Dow Jones in his home city of Melbourne over the Internet version of its weekly financial magazine *Barron's*. The magazine had 550,000 subscribers internationally, of whom only 1700 had Australia-based credit cards. Well known UK-based lawyer Geoffrey Robertson QC argued for the publisher that the article had been 'published from' New Jersey when it was 'uploaded', but the court ruled it was actually published every time it was 'downloaded' anywhere throughout the world. The decision gave Gutnick the right to sue for defamation in Victoria, his place of primary residence and the location where he was best known.

In the same year as the *Gutnick* decision, a New York District Court considered whether material was actually 'published' when it was posted to the Internet. In *Getaped. com Inc v Cangemi*, a motor scooter business claimed parts of its website had been copied. Cangemi argued the website was not a publication, but rather a 'public display' or performance. But Judge Alvin Hellerstein said, 'when a webpage goes live on the Internet, it is distributed and "published".'[4]

▶ The long arm of cyberlaw

The *Dow Jones v Gutnick* decision shows just how long the arm of cyberlaw can be. In that case it stretched all the way from Melbourne, Australia, to allow a businessman to take suit against a publisher based in New Jersey, in the US. The same kind of thing happened in 2011, when a Californian court ordered US-based Twitter to hand over the name, contact details and location of a British-based local government councillor whom South Tyneside Council had accused of anonymously posting defamatory comments.

When lawyers talk about the 'where' element of an action, the legal term they use is 'jurisdiction'. The word can have a range of legal meanings, but for our purposes it applies to the location of your publication and whether a particular country's laws or courts have any authority over it—and you.

Early last century that was all fairly straightforward. Most media organisations were focused on audiences within well-defined geographical areas. Publishers and readers were covered by the same laws and court systems— at provincial and national levels. Even when a television network broadcast or a newspaper circulated across state borders, the media companies and their lawyers were usually only dealing with two sets of laws. However, the second half of the twentieth century introduced interstate and international media organisations—national daily newspapers such as *USA Today* and international broadcasters such as CNN and BBC World. Now, with the advent of the Internet and social media, you have to consider the legal implications of publishing everywhere, every time you upload your writing.

This does not mean the security police from a remote regime are likely to come knocking on the doors of bloggers in western democracies, arresting and extraditing you for punishment under their traditional systems of law. They do not normally have the legal authority to act outside their own borders. However, you might be called to account for your postings under their laws if you happen to travel there. And citizens in other countries can go to court and get a declaration against you in your absence, perhaps ordering you to pay a certain sum in damages for something you have published.

That happened to US citizen Bill White in 2003 after he had posted numerous highly defamatory allegations against former colleague Dr Trevor Cullen and others. Each time White's defamatory websites were taken down as the result of complaints, White had changed Internet service providers (ISPs) and published them again. Cullen took his action to the Supreme Court in his home state of Western Australia and won a declaratory judgment of $95,000. White did not defend the case and the damages had not been paid at the time of his death in 2004.[5]

Under international treaties, nations with equivalent laws to those in your own country can seek to extradite you from your homeland to face trial and punishment for serious publishing offences such as the trafficking of child pornography or terrorism. This means foreign governments and lawyers might seek information about you from ISPs or social media networks based in another country, even for non-criminal actions such as defamation or privacy infringement.

▶ How hospitable is your host?

While the strict letter of international law might not give a country power to act, some governments and litigants put pressure on ISPs and multinational websites over content. For example, in late 2010 YouTube took down footage of a Turkish politician in a hotel bedroom with a female staffer after an Ankara court declared the video-sharing website would be blocked in Turkey if it did not comply.[6] In another case, Yahoo! Holdings in Hong Kong surrendered information to Chinese authorities about reporter Shi Tao, who worked for the daily *Dangdai Shang Bao* (Contemporary Business News). He was jailed for ten years from 2005 for 'divulging state secrets abroad'. In 2008, the heavy equipment rental company Gremach sued Google's Indian subsidiary for defamation[7] and obtained an order from the Bombay High Court demanding Google reveal the identity of an anonymous blogger called 'Toxic Writer' who had criticised Gremach on Google's platform Blogger.com.

Internet service providers' commitment to protecting users from hostile civil and criminal actions seems to vary according to where they are based and the commercial and political pressures of the moment. While some will take a stand on your behalf in the name of Internet freedom and privacy, you can never rely on them to keep your identity secret.

▶ Who carries the can?

Most bloggers cherish their independence, but this comes at a price. If you are the sole publisher of your material, then prosecutors and litigants will come looking for you personally. If you write for a larger organisation you share responsibility with your employer or client. A litigant can still sue you as the writer, but they might choose to target your wealthier publisher—particularly if you are an impoverished freelancer.

In the twentieth century, large media organisations would usually provide in-house counsel to guide their journalists through any civil or criminal actions, as well as pay any legal costs and damages.

Most of the so-called 'legacy media' still do this today, so if you are a mainstream reporter or columnist thinking of going solo with your blog you might weigh this up first. Another advantage of writing for a large media group is that your work will be checked by editors with some legal knowledge and perhaps even vetted by the company's lawyers before being published. Either way, you might investigate insuring yourself against civil damages, although even in countries where this is possible premiums are rising with each new Internet lawsuit. Another option is to scout for liability insurance policies offered by authors' and bloggers' associations. Check out your options.

ISPs and providers of publishing platforms such as Twitter usually escape liability for their users' content, especially if they remain ignorant of its illegality. But jurisdictions vary on whether ISPs become responsible for the material once they have been informed that it is criminal or that it infringes upon someone's rights.

▶ Status update: it's posted and you're liable

The law might require your posting to reach just one other person for you to become legally liable for its content. (In the case of libel, it needs to be a third person beyond you and the person you are defaming.) You might think you are just corresponding with your cosy group of Twitter followers or Facebook friends—all with a shared sense of humour—but your remark can go viral very quickly when it is forwarded, retweeted or picked up by the mainstream media. That's exactly what happened when lawyer and academic Larissa Behrendt saw Indigenous Australian spokeswoman Bess Price appear on ABC television soon after watching a particularly graphic episode of *Deadwood*. She tweeted to her followers: 'I watched a show where a guy had sex with a horse and I'm sure it was less offensive than Bess Price.' As soon as the comments reached the mainstream media, Price threatened to sue. Behrendt apologised.[8]

The lesson for us as bloggers or social media users is that our communication in cyberspace is not like chatting with a group of friends at a café. As soon as our postings come to the attention of our 'victims' or the authorities, the courts will hold us responsible for the original publication. Third parties will also be liable if they forward our message to others, but our responsibility for the act of publication rests with our first post.

Courts will consider the extent of republication when assessing damages. Sadly, if your words have gone viral you are likely to face a larger damages payout. But if others add to your words with more inflammatory material of their own, they carry responsibility for the new publication. Think twice before retweeting or forwarding the legally dubious material of others, because doing so makes it a new publication under your own name; at the very least you will share the legal liability with the original publisher. It is poor social media practice to retweet, 'like' or forward anything without first reviewing it thoroughly. That defamatory or criminal material might just be in the final paragraph of the article you have blindly re-sent, and you are suddenly liable for republishing it. The same has been applied to embedded links in your postings, particularly to criminal material. Some people have been held responsible for their hyperlinks to the offensive words of others.[9] Canadian bloggers can rest a little easier, though. The Canadian Supreme Court ruled in 2011 that links to defamatory material will normally be safe as long as the libel is not in the actual letters of the URL.[10]

▶ Are you being criminal, or just uncivil?

Lawyers and prosecutors will of course look closely at what you have published to decide whether your work is a criminal offence or might be subject to a civil suit. It is important to distinguish between these areas of the law.

Online publishers who commit crimes may face fines and a range of other punishments, which can include (depending on the country) execution, corporal punishment such as caning, imprisonment and community service. Serious publication crimes internationally include sedition, contempt of court or parliament, criminal libel, hate speech, breach of publishing restrictions, unlicensed publishing, fraud and various national security breaches.

Civil actions involve other people or corporations suing you for such things as defamation, breach of privacy, breach of confidentiality, misrepresentation, breach of copyright and breach of contract. If you lose a civil suit a court will order you to pay damages to the plaintiff or demand that you change your behaviour in some way. Judges do this by issuing an injunction to do—or refrain from doing—something. Such orders might insist you publish an apology or that you remove material from your website. Breaching or ignoring such an order becomes a criminal matter.

▶ Threats aren't always legal

Just because someone disagrees with your publication—even if they are upset or embarrassed by it—does not in itself mean you have done something illegal. Your criminal and civil liability will depend upon whether there is a law controlling that kind of publication in a jurisdiction where you can be charged or sued.

Throughout the world a range of online material has been the subject of legal action. This has included the publication of words, symbols, still and moving images, sounds, illustrations, headlines, captions and links. Sometimes it is the very words alone that are banned, such as the name of a victim of a sex crime, while on other occasions it is the overall coverage that creates a meaning that damages a reputation—such as a photograph of someone accompanying a negative story. Many of these types of material are associated with particular laws. For example, the unauthorised use of brands or symbols is dealt with under trademark law; the original expression of an idea is protected by copyright law; limits on what we can say about others are determined by defamation laws; and there are even laws in many jurisdictions dealing with the ancient offences of blasphemy or lese-majesty. In some countries the simple act of publishing without an official permit is banned.

▶ **Time works for and against us ...**

Time warps on the Internet. It is one of the most important aspects of new media, and one of the most complicating in legal terms. On the one hand, pressing the Send or Publish button makes your work instant and irretrievable. While the newspaper publisher could always pulp an offensive edition before the trucks left the factory, as a blogger or microblogger you have to live with the consequences of your digital publishing errors. Yes, you can remove your blog, tweet or Facebook status within seconds of posting it, and request that it be taken down from search engines. But you can never be sure someone hasn't captured, downloaded and forwarded it in the meantime.

This permanent quality of new media does not mix well with an online writer's impulsiveness, carelessness or substance abuse. There is an old saying: 'Doctors bury their mistakes. Lawyers jail theirs. But journalists publish theirs for all the world to see.' That can be applied to anyone writing online today. At least in bygone times these mistakes would gradually fade from memory. While they might linger in the yellowing editions of newspapers in library archives, it would take a keen researcher to find them several years later. Now your offensive or erroneous writing is only a Google search away for anyone motivated to look.

British actor Stephen Fry learned this in 2010 when he tweeted his two million followers, insulting *Telegraph* journalist Milo Yiannopoulos over a critical column. 'Fry quickly deleted the tweet once others started to latch on to it, but as we know that rarely helps when you've posted something injudicious online: the Internet remembers,' Yiannopoulos wrote.[11]

This new permanence of stored material also creates problems for digital archives[12]—because if the material remains on the publisher's servers it may be considered 'republished' each time it is downloaded. This means that even where there might be some statutory time limitation on lawsuits, the clock starts ticking again with each download, so you don't get to take advantage of the time limit until you have removed the material from your site. The best policy is to take all steps to withdraw any dubious material as soon as possible. If others choose to forward or republish it, it has hopefully become their problem rather than yours.

▶ Is your blog 'in the public interest' or just 'interesting to the public'?

Lawyers, prosecutors and judges will also look to your motives for publishing the material you have written. In some places those motives can actually form a defence, while on other occasions your motives can be your undoing. But two are worth considering here because of their very different impact on the law: public interest and malice.

Many statutes and court rulings use the expression 'public interest' as an element of a defence to a range of publishing crimes and civil wrongs. In such matters you would have to convince the court that some greater public good came from the material you published and that society benefited in some way as a result. You would normally need to show that any public benefit outweighed the harm that was caused by the publication, which is normally the reason you are called to account. For example, your defence to a defamation action might be that it was in the public interest that your audience learned of your corruption allegations against a leading politician, even if you could not quite prove that the allegations were true.

Sometimes the words 'public interest' are not used, but the defence itself has come from a balancing of public interests against other rights. For example, copyright law in most countries has a range of 'fair use' defences so that parts of copyright material can be republished for the purposes of education, news or critique. The defences exist because politicians have decided that there is a greater 'public interest' in the community being educated and informed about such important matters than in protecting the intellectual property owned by the creator of the work. However, as many judges have pointed out, 'public interest' does not equate with 'interesting to the public', and you should not be allowed to destroy someone's reputation or invade their privacy simply because your gossip is particularly saucy.

By far the best-known right to free expression is the First Amendment to the US Constitution. It states: 'Congress shall make no law . . . abridging the freedom of speech, or of the press.' The US Supreme Court has interpreted the First Amendment very broadly and has applied it across media to a whole range of publishing situations. It certainly applies to the material bloggers, Facebook users and tweeters create there—particularly if you are commenting on matters of public importance.

In a series of decisions throughout the twentieth century the Supreme Court allowed newspapers and broadcasters to use the First Amendment to bolster their defences against laws affecting their publications. This was especially useful in defamation law, where a defence allows the media to publish libellous material about a public figure as long as they do not know it is false and they are not being malicious.

The First Amendment is so entrenched in US society that bloggers sometimes operate under the assumption that this same protection will apply in other parts of the world. Unfortunately, it does not.

▶ Absence of malice

The motivation that will ruin almost any defence in a publishing case is malice. Even the US, which has one of the strongest defamation defences in the world under its First Amendment protection, will not excuse a slur against somebody if it can be proven to be false and malicious.

'Malice' has a wide range of definitions in international law. In some places it is interpreted very narrowly, along the lines of its lay definition in *Cambridge Dictionaries Online*: 'the wish to harm or upset other people'. Elsewhere the definition becomes quite complex and can take in a less spiteful objective, such as going ahead with a publication when you know the allegation is false or while 'recklessly disregarding' whether the material is true or not. Your online behaviour can also be used as evidence in court. Lawyers will dig around for all kinds of evidence that you have been less than honest about your behaviour, or have shown malice or a lack of good faith in your dealings.

These are the types of issues journalists have dealt with for generations. Perhaps as a blogger or a social media user you see yourself as a 'citizen journalist', or perhaps you object to that description. Either way, a court will look to your motivation for publishing an item. If you can lay claim to some overriding public interest and show that you have made proper and fair enquiries before publishing your material, you may not have a watertight defence but you will be much better placed than those who do not think twice before they inject their latest dose of venom into cyberspace.

▶ There's a message in the medium

Your method and your medium can be important factors in your legal exposure. The simple fact is that some publishing mechanisms are more law-friendly than others. Sometimes this will depend on the type of material you are publishing.

For example, Twitter users may be less prone to copyright infringement because the 140-character limit on each posting restricts the amount of another person's work they can borrow, and the retweeting function implies that everyone expects their work to be recycled by others. However, on Twitter you leave yourself more exposed in the area of defamation because there is so little space for you to give context and balance to your criticism of others. Longer, better-argued critiques are more likely to attract the fair comment defences in many countries. Tweeting from an event as it unfolds, such as a conference or a court case, has its dangers, because your tweets might contain errors in the quotes of others or might be taken out of context by someone reading a single tweet rather than the overall coverage. And of course most of us tweet with the full expectation that our work will be spread far and wide, meaning any libellous material can cause considerable damage.

Publication on Facebook, however, might be restricted to just a few friends, particularly if your privacy settings are adjusted so that your comments are not viewable to the friends of your friends. The open blog has a potentially wide distribution network, but there are quite prudent controls available to you when you use a host such as WordPress. You should take advantage of opportunities to save drafts and proofread your material in preview mode before proceeding to publication. Careful checking before publication can help you find accidental spelling mistakes and remind you of extra fact-checking you will need to carry out before pressing that magic button.

If you write fairly and accurately it can go a long way to establishing a defence to defamation. Blogging is also about writing quality, so your mastery of language and your selection of the most appropriate words can be crucial when defending a libel allegation—for example, if you have written a scathing review of a public event or performance.

You might take a moment to look over some of your recent blogs, tweets and Facebook postings. How well do they shape up? And who is that knocking at your front door? ;-)

IN BRIEF: BASIC RISKS

- In the eyes of the law, you are published whenever and wherever someone downloads your work.

- Criminal and civil laws apply as much to bloggers and social media users as they do to large media corporations.

- Don't post anything unless you're comfortable with it going public—well beyond your cosy friendship group.

- Never forward or retweet material or links without reading and viewing them first.

- If you're an American citizen, don't kid yourself that the First Amendment protects your material beyond US borders.

- Courts will often look to whether your work is 'in the public interest'.

- Don't get nasty or sloppy. Malice defeats many defences.

- Think about the legal risks of the medium you are using. Some carry more dangers than others in certain situations.

CHAPTER 2

CYBERLIBEL AND REPUTATIONAL DAMAGE ONLINE

Twitbrief: Paying the price for venting about others online. Defamation laws and defences at home and abroad. #libel #damages #1stAmend #truth #malice

Up-and-coming fashion designer Dawn Simorangkir was delighted when she was asked to create some clothing for Courtney Love in 2008. But she could never have guessed she would be receiving a US$430,000 settlement from the rock celebrity three years later. Love was furious when Simorangkir sent her an invoice for her creations under the Boudoir Queen label. The troubled star fired off scores of blog and Twitter rants,[1] accusing the designer of being a thief, burglar, felon, drug addict, prostitute, embezzler, cocaine dealer and an unfit mother. By mid-2011, Love had issued an unconditional apology as part of a mediated court settlement, only to find her former lawyers had filed suit over another series of tweets, in which she had claimed they had taken a bribe.[2]

Love was the latest in a long line of bloggers and social media users to learn that defamation can be just as damaging online as it is in the traditional media—and just as expensive. The Love case also shows that defamation is a risk for all online writers, even in the US with its strong traditions of free speech.

▶ Thin skins the world over

'Defamation' is the legal term for reputational damage and it applies in one form or another throughout most of the world. It is the most common area of litigation for writers of all kinds across new and old media and is one of the main legal pitfalls for you as a blogger or microblogger.

Defamation terminology and laws vary across different countries. You will sometimes see defamation referred to as 'libel' (its permanently published form) or 'slander' (when spoken). Mass-media products, websites, blogs and social media postings fall into the 'libel' category in countries that make this distinction.

Defamation is usually actioned as a 'tort'—the area of the law where a citizen can file suit against another over a 'civil wrong' that has been done to them. If they win, courts will usually award them a sum of damages in compensation or make some other order—perhaps stopping the publication or forcing an apology.

▶ Go directly to jail

You can still be jailed or fined in some places for 'criminal defamation'. In some countries criminal libel or 'seditious libel' (defamation of the state) is used as a tool of censorship against the media and dissidents by politicians, business leaders and government officials.

Criminal defamation still exists in many liberal democracies, including the US and Australia, but prosecutions are rare and are usually reserved for poisonous, malicious attacks on someone's character by a person who lacks the money to pay damages—someone the courts have called a 'man of straw'. University of Northern Colorado law student Thomas Mink thought it was amusing when he published a satirical online newsletter called *The Howling Pig* in 2003, featuring a photo of finance academic Junius Peake altered to look like KISS guitarist Gene Simmons. He captioned it 'Mr Junius Puke'. Professor Peake was not amused. Police confiscated Mink's computer under warrant and jailed him for a week under Colorado's criminal libel laws. It was not until 2011 that the student won a lawsuit against the deputy district attorney who had issued the warrant, on the grounds that the seizure and arrest were unconstitutional.[3]

▶ Suits from governments, companies and zombies

In some countries corporations and government agencies can sue for defamation, while elsewhere only private citizens can bring a libel action. Related actions such as 'injurious falsehood' or 'trade libel' are available to corporations— with a higher burden of proof on plaintiffs (those doing the suing).

Even the dead can sue in some jurisdictions—or at least their relatives can sue over reputational damage you have caused their surviving family and the memory of the deceased.

We will look at some of these differences and how they have played out in recent cases when we consider the major jurisdictions a little later. For the moment, let's consider some of the broad-brush principles of defamation that apply in most parts of the world today.

▶ Losing face on Facebook

Defamation law everywhere requires proof that your publication has lowered someone's standing in the eyes of at least one other person. It must go to this third person before the 'reputation' can be damaged, because your reputation is your standing in the eyes of others. In other words, if you insult someone in a direct message (DM) to them alone on Twitter, you have not defamed them. But if you repeat the slur to just one other tweep your victim might then have an action in defamation.

We have all seen how a major newspaper or television network can destroy someone's reputation in an instant, but you might have felt comfortable saying what you like about someone to your handful of blog followers or your twenty Facebook friends. Sorry, but as soon as you say something nasty about someone to a single Facebook friend or your only Twitter follower, you have defamed the victim of your comments. Most of the time this will just cause a little embarrassment to both you and them if they find out, but occasionally a single publication to just one other person can be devastating—and expensive.

The name David Milum might not be familiar to you, but he was a pioneer in defamation law—for all the wrong reasons. He ran a political website in Forsyth County, Georgia, and became the first US blogger to lose a libel case when in 2004 he wrote that an attorney had delivered bribes from drug dealers to a judge.[4] The appeal court held in 2007 that bloggers and podcasters were just as liable for defamation action as other publishers and the attorney won US$50,000 in damages.

Courts can award substantial damages to someone who has been injured in some way because of your nasty posting. Perhaps they have been traumatised, their relationships have been damaged or they have lost a lucrative contract. Even the fact that you didn't mean to defame them will not necessarily protect you. In most countries only your act of publication needs to be intentional, not your intent to damage the person's reputation. There are several exceptions to this. For example, ISPs are usually not liable for defamation on the websites they host unless the material has been brought to their attention and they have refused to take it down. In the US, this goes further: section 230 of the *Communications Decency Act* gives full protection to 'interactive computer services', even protecting blog hosts from liability for comments by users.[5] Careful here, though, because users can be sued over their comments if they are identifiable via their IP (Internet protocol) addresses—and the host might cough yours up.

Bloggers often mistakenly think their ISP or host site would be sued for defamation instead of them. Lancashire academic Tracy Williams used a pseudonym to defame a UK Independence Party candidate on a Yahoo! discussion board in 2004. She called him a sexual offender, a racist bigot and a Nazi, and escalated her abuse when he started legal action. The politician won a court order against Yahoo! forcing the company to reveal her identity, and in 2006 she became the first blogger to lose a libel action in the UK High Court. It cost her £10,000 in damages.[6] And in 2011 Twitter was ordered by a Californian court to reveal to South Tyneside Council in the UK the personal details of the users behind five accounts who had allegedly defamed three of its councillors.[7]

▶ **Are you responsible?**

Anyone having direct responsibility for a publication is legally liable for it, so if your blog is on the website of another organisation, both you as the writer and the corporation hosting your work can be targeted in a defamation suit. If someone edits your work before it is published, they too share the burden of legal liability. And if anyone republishes your work, through syndication or perhaps even through retweeting or forwarding, they are also liable. As noted in Chapter 1, even someone who inserts a hyperlink to libellous material can be sued for defamation in some places.[8]

Plaintiffs will sue any of these people or organisations for a range of reasons. Sometimes they just want to gag the discussion, so they issue a defamation writ to chill the criticism. This is known as a 'SLAPP' writ—'Strategic Lawsuits Against Public Participation'—and in some countries they are simply thrown out of court as an affront to free expression. Others allow them. Plaintiffs often want to get the highest possible damages award from someone who can afford to pay it, so they might bypass the original, impoverished blogger and sue the wealthier company that republished the material. Sometimes they enjoin all of them in their action, although this adds to their legal costs if they lose.

▶ Name and shame?

As we learned from the *Gutnick* case in the previous chapter, publication happens whenever and wherever someone downloads the material in question. If you have published something defamatory about someone who is unknown in your own state or country you are probably out of their reach until you travel to the place where they do have a reputation.

The person claiming defamation would have to prove they could be identified from the material you posted. Of course, if you have named somebody they are identifiable, but what if you use other identifiers? For example, what if your blog questioned the ability of 'a prominent 21st Avenue cosmetic surgeon responsible for the fat lips and lopsided breasts of at least three Oscar winners'? You would be much better off to take legal advice first, and perhaps to actually name the surgeon if you have a solid defence available to you. Why? Because there might well be other surgeons who meet this description, and you would have a hard time defending a suit from them if you didn't even know they existed.

If your description is broad enough you will normally be reasonably safe. So if you had made your description fairly general—'an LA cosmetic surgeon'—the group would be too large for any single surgeon to be able to prove you were talking about them. (They say there are almost as many cosmetic surgeons as lawyers in LA!)

Of course, if you decide after taking legal advice to actually name someone, you need to ensure you use enough identifiers to ensure they will not be mistaken for someone else. That's why court reports in the news usually state the full name, suburb, occupation and age of an accused person. Otherwise someone by the same name might show that their reputation was damaged, by proving their friends and colleagues thought they were the rapist, murderer or drug dealer you were writing about.

▶ **That's ridiculous!**

Defamatory material can be almost anything you publish—words, images, sounds or gestures. In a recent German case, where Daimler employees insulted their boss on a social media protest page, a court found even a Facebook thumbs-up 'Like' symbol was enough to qualify as a defamatory statement.[9] The defamatory meaning might be very clear through the use of derogatory words, like those used by Courtney Love in her postings about that fashion designer. But the meaning can also come from what the courts call 'innuendo'—inside knowledge that only a select few people might know about the person, or meanings that come from reading between the lines. Saying the church leader is not someone you would invite to your child's pyjama party could easily be interpreted as an accusation that they are a paedophile.

The courts have to decide whether your material might make other ordinary citizens think less of this person, shun or avoid them, expose them to hatred or contempt—or even just hold them up to ridicule. It's easy to imagine the kinds of things you might write about someone that would cause others to hate or avoid them: calling them a criminal, a sex offender, a cheat, unprofessional, negligent, uncaring or unreliable are just a few examples. But ridiculing them—or prompting others to laugh at their expense—can also be defamatory. Many blogs and social media postings try to be humorous or witty, so it is common for them to ask their readers to have a giggle at someone. This might take the form of an amusing video clip, a nickname you have coined for them, manipulating their image to make them look silly, or by inventing some fictional scenario with them as the lead character. The possibilities are almost endless, but unfortunately so are the real-life defamation cases that have resulted from them.

Sometimes the defamation stems from the placement of the material on the page or the website. You might have a perfectly acceptable story about someone, but adjacent material might make them look ridiculous or suspicious—the ad for the airline next to the story about a jet crash; or the heading about impotence treatment above the photo of the ageing actor.

▶ In my defence, your honour . . .

All this has probably sent you into a state of shock, particularly if you only just uploaded that defamatory blog post before reading this chapter. By this stage you must be asking whether it is worthwhile blogging or participating in social media at all if you can never be critical of others or have a little fun. The fact is an enormous amount of defamatory material is published safely on the Internet each day. Some of it is safe because the person posting the material is either anonymous or beyond the legal reach of the victim. Some is safe because the person targeted has little reputation to defend. Sometimes it is just that the victim lacks either the resources or the will to embark on the whole legal process of a defamation suit. And often it is because there is a rock-solid defence

available to the writer or publisher who has created or
posted the material.

The defences vary considerably between nations and
jurisdictions within them, and we will look at some of
those differences later. Much depends on the level of free
expression in a particular country. Regions with strong
constitutional protections of free speech, such as North
America and Scandinavia, offer generous defamation
defences. Countries with heavy censorship regimes lack
even some of the basic defences or place a burden of
proof on defendants to justify their publications, often
without even the basic entitlements of natural justice.

▶ The truth is out there ... but try proving it

Most western democracies allow truth as a defence to
defamation, although in most places it is not as easy to
prove as it might sound. It is usually a defence of 'strict
liability'—meaning the defendant has to prove the truth of
the allegation rather than the plaintiff having the burden
of proving its falsity. In some places plaintiffs carry this
burden if they are public figures who should expect some
criticism of their lives and performance.

Proving truth is not as easy as it seems because it
requires you to provide the court with evidence that
meets its rules of admissibility. This complicates things
for the blogger or cyberjournalist who uses confidential
sources. If you want to keep the identity of those sources
secret, they are not much help in proving the truth of
your serious allegations because they will be unwilling to
appear as witnesses in court or identify themselves in a
legally admissible statement. Admissibility questions arise
over a range of evidence types—copies of documents you

have obtained where the court cannot sight the originals; images or sound recordings obtained deceptively; and the testimony of sources who have since died, moved or are now unwilling to testify. Many a defamation defendant has been left high and dry, certain of the truth of what they wrote but unable to produce enough evidence to convince a judge or jury.

It is not normally sufficient that you prove you are truthfully quoting someone else's defamatory remarks. Unless they were speaking on a specially protected occasion, the truth defence would normally require you to prove the factual truth of what they said because you are effectively republishing their words. That's another reason to be very careful before you retweet, forward or 'Like' someone else's work. Read it first and assess it as though it is your own publication—because as soon as you press Send, it becomes your own work in the eyes of the law.

Another problem with truth is that the courts might require you to prove more than the bare facts you have published—they might also insist you prove the truth of any implied defamatory meaning coming from those facts. For example, you might have the facts to prove that millions of dollars have gone missing from a major company—and that its accountant has recently resigned and purchased a luxury cruiser and a private jet in the Bahamas—but the truth defence will usually require you to prove the defamatory meaning ('imputation') coming from this set of facts: that the accountant stole the money. This is a much greater challenge and requires considerably more evidence, such as bank transactions, witness statements or admissible recordings of confessions.

All that said, if the defamation action is a civil lawsuit rather than a criminal prosecution, you will only need to convince a judge or jury under the civil legal burden of proof—on the 'balance of probabilities'—rather than the tough criminal law requirement of 'beyond reasonable doubt'. Defamation laws often state that they require the defendant only to prove the 'substantial truth' of their allegations, which again implies something short of a comprehensive brief of evidence.

When you take all this into account, as a wise blogger or social media user you should seek legal advice before rushing to publication under the assumption that you have truth on your side.

▶ Opinion and satire

Lawyers and judges in different countries will use different words to describe it, but there is usually a defamation defence available for your fair expression of critical opinion on a matter of public interest. Some jurisdictions offer protection to satirical and humorous depictions of prominent people and their work, and some even allow parodies or impersonations of public figures and their creations. We will look more closely at this later when we cover identity in Chapter 4 and intellectual property in Chapter 8.

Most liberal democracies will allow quite harsh criticism of almost anything in the public arena under defences called 'fair comment' or 'honest opinion'. They are based on the idea that anyone who has a public role or who puts their work out into a public forum should expect it to be criticised or even lampooned by others. This is exactly what happens on blogs and social media networks, so it can be a very useful defence. To earn it you will normally need to ensure that the target of your critique is indeed in the public domain. This would cover criticism of such things as the quality and service of hotels and restaurants; reviews of creative works such as music, books and artworks; critiques of sports and entertainment performances; and reflections on the role and statements of politicians and other public officials. Reviews of private matters, such as the karaoke performance of a guest at your friend's wedding reception, would normally not qualify because they are not public events.

Your defamatory material would need to be your honest opinion, based upon provable facts that are stated in the material. Evidence of malicious intent on your part would normally defeat the fair comment defence.

Reviewers of music or accommodation use this defence for quite strong criticism, although sometimes even they find themselves at the wrong end of a defamation suit. That happened to two travellers who wrote a review on the popular travel site TripAdvisor, claiming an Illinois hotel had bedbugs. The hotel insisted the allegation was false, and launched a US$30,000 defamation action.[10]

While facts might be provable, you obviously cannot prove the truth or falsity of opinions, which are subjective in their nature. In the US, the Supreme Court has ruled that opinions on public matters are totally protected from defamation because opinions cannot be proven false. But even there the law will not allow you to parade a fact as an opinion. For example, you could not write, 'In my opinion, Jones is a rapist and the judge must be demented.' In such a case, the court would view both allegations as statements of fact, and you would need to prove the truth of each. However, if you had drawn on provable facts to prove Jones had indeed committed serious sexual offences and had just been convicted of rape, you might write your honest opinion.

You might write something like: 'The one-year jail sentence Jones received for this rape is grossly inadequate. It is hard to imagine how someone who has caused such damage to this woman will walk free in just twelve months. Judge Brown's sentencing decision is mind-boggling and out of all proportion to sentences by other judges for similar crimes. His appointment is up for renewal in February and, if this sentence is any indication, it is high time he retired.' You can express a very strong opinion within the bounds of this defence as long as you are basing your comments on a foundation of provable facts.

The defence might not be as well suited to material published on Twitter because the 140 available characters offer so little space for you to show the factual framework upon which you are basing your libellous opinion. Either way, you should hold back and seek legal advice if there is a risk your opinion might be seen as unfair, dishonest or malicious, based upon false facts, or on a private rather than a public matter.

▶ **Protected reports**

You are also usually allowed to publish defamatory material in fair and accurate reports of certain important public forums, such as the proceedings of a court or parliament. Depending on the jurisdiction, other occasions such as local government meetings, public meetings and tribunal hearings might be covered by a similar defence, although the defence is normally strongest for reports of court or parliamentary proceedings. These are the occasions when witnesses and other people speaking or tabling documents have complete immunity ('absolute privilege') against defamation action for anything they say or documents they table. Those reporting their libellous testimony to the broader public win a limited protection from defamation as long as their coverage is 'fair' and their reports are accurate.

Sometimes 'fairness' requires that the report is published reasonably soon after the proceedings—you might lose the defence if you post it long after the community has forgotten about the case. The overall coverage needs to be fair as well. You would not have the defence available if you just chose the most sensational and damaging part of a court hearing or a parliamentary debate without giving the reader the broader context of the debate, including anything said in the defence of the person defamed. Serious errors in your coverage—such as attributing the material to the wrong person or wrongly identifying the person who is the subject of the defamatory slur—will normally lose the defence.

One of the biggest problems facing the online writer and publisher is whether the defamation protection of such proceedings extends to other jurisdictions. It could be the situation that the law in your country offers the defence for coverage of local proceedings but does not extend it to coverage of foreign courts or parliaments. This might mean that the aggrieved person or company could sue you in another jurisdiction where you have published the material.

▶ Public interest and public figures

Many jurisdictions offer a 'public interest' or 'qualified privilege' defence for defamatory material about extremely important public issues, where the publisher might not have quite enough evidence available to prove truth and other defences might not apply. It's important to distinguish here between matters of legitimate 'public interest' and other matters, such as celebrity gossip, which might be just 'interesting to the public'. Even so, under special protections in the US you can get away with false publications about celebrities and other public figures as long as you are not being malicious in your attacks. Again, you need to be wary of less forgiving laws in other places, particularly if the celebrity has a reputation they wish to defend elsewhere—like the Australian actress Nicole Kidman or the New Zealand filmmaker Peter Jackson.

In other countries the public interest or qualified privilege defence normally requires you to show that you acted in good faith and made proper enquiries in the lead-up to your defamatory publication, despite being unable to prove its truth. Journalists may be better positioned to make use of this defence than so-called 'citizen journalists' or amateur bloggers because they have been trained in research skills and verification practices. However, there has been little to indicate that bloggers or social media users will not qualify for the defence. In fact, the Minnesota District Court granted Republican blogger Michael Brodkorb the same rights as a traditional reporter not to be sued by public figures when he cited an anonymous source to accuse a Democratic political advisor of self-interest.[11]

▶ 'Sorry' seems to be the hardest word ...

Sometimes we just screw up. You should get legal advice the instant someone threatens you with a defamation suit. The laws in some countries reward fast and prominent apologies and offers of financial settlement. In fact, in the UK[12] and Australia[13] an early offer of amends in settlement is a complete defence to defamation if the plaintiff decides to pursue the matter regardless and a court later finds the original offer was reasonable. But even there the offer has to meet technical requirements and is best handled by a lawyer. Rash or poorly worded apologies can sometimes go wrong and escalate the matter further or erode your chance of arguing one of the defences. While you might feel the moral urge to apologise, it is best to run the wording past your lawyer first.

▶ Damages, injunctions and declarations

The most common remedy for defamation is an award of damages to compensate your victim for their emotional hurt and any financial loss they might have suffered from your posting. This can range from a pittance through to millions. Just as damaging can be the lawyers' fees and court costs, which can escalate immeasurably with appeals and delays.

In some countries courts can award huge damages. In 2006, a jury ordered a Louisiana woman to pay US$11.3 million to a Florida woman for website forum postings claiming she was a 'crook', a 'con artist' and a 'fraud'.[14] Other jurisdictions, such as Australia, cap the damages courts can award for non-economic loss.

Judges also have the power to issue injunctions—court orders—preventing the publication of defamatory material or insisting that already published items be removed. Courts in freer countries have been reluctant to gag publications because of a centuries-old principle against 'prior restraint'. Leading politicians and jurists have decried the idea of censoring material before publication by way of injunctions and publishing licences. Instead, they prefer a system where defamatory material can be dealt with by court action after it has been published so there is minimal censorship prior to publication. While judges have generally followed this principle, there have been many exceptions where they have previewed defamatory material and issued injunctions to stop media organisations going ahead with their release. These are known as 'gag orders' or 'stop writs'.

A less common remedy is for the plaintiff simply to request the court to issue a 'declaration of falsehood' about untruths that have been published about them. British novelist Salman Rushdie won such a declaration in 2008 against a former police officer who wrote a memoir about his time guarding Rushdie during his years in fatwa exile.[15] The book contained eleven statements that the court acknowledged as untrue. The original edition was pulped and the book was withdrawn from sale while the changes were made. The writer and publisher apologised and they paid Rushdie's court costs of several thousand pounds. He said he did not pursue a damages award because he was opposed in principle to the chilling effect of damages upon free speech.

▶ Defamation region by region

The following paragraphs set out the definitions and implications of reputation damage globally.

UK and Commonwealth countries

Defamation laws throughout the UK and its former colonies are a mix of centuries-old case law (the 'common law') and legislation. The UK courts have had some of their decisions challenged via the European Convention on Human Rights and have also seen a recent push for libel reform. But the guiding principles of defamation remain similar across most places in the world formerly coloured British Empire-red on the world map. Most draw upon English case law for their definitions of defamation and offer the basic defences we have covered: truth, protected reporting, fair comment and qualified privilege (public interest). Most also still have criminal libel on their statutes, and sadly this is used to prosecute journalists and dissidents far too frequently in smaller regimes throughout Africa and the Pacific.

A Western Australian case was one of the world's first instances of defamation over the Internet. The 1994 *Rindos v Hardwick* case involved allegations of sexual misconduct, racist attitudes and incompetence against an anthropology academic that were transmitted via a computer bulletin board.[16] The plaintiff won $40,000 in damages.

Canadian defamation law is in general accord with the British, except in Quebec, where there is a strong French influence and some of the European civil law principles are followed.

Cases and law reforms in some Commonwealth countries have introduced guidelines of 'responsible journalism' for publishers wanting to take advantage of the qualified privilege (public interest) defence when the material proved to be false. These were outlined by the

House of Lords in the *Reynolds* case in 1999[17] and in the reformed uniform *Defamation Act* in Australian states and territories in 2005–6. The Supreme Court of Canada developed a defence of 'responsible communication' in 2009.[18] It stemmed from a *Toronto Star* article claiming that property developer Peter Grant was pulling political strings in his efforts to get a golf course approved. He sued for libel over the allegation and the court decided there should be a defence for publications on a matter of public interest that are properly researched, even if they are proven to be false. Importantly, they extended the defence to non-journalist bloggers.[19]

Throughout the 1990s several countries—including Australia, New Zealand, South Africa and India—extended their defamation defences to allow a greater freedom to communicate on political and government matters.[20]

United States

These international moves to reform defamation laws to allow for more criticism of political figures and discussion of important public issues came almost half a century after the US Supreme Court decided the First Amendment should offer better defamation defences. Basic principles in US law had generally followed the British common law until the 1960s, and they still share many common ideas.

A landmark US case, *New York Times v Sullivan,*[21] was decided in 1964. An elected Alabama official claimed the newspaper had defamed him by publishing an advertisement that alleged police under his supervision had been violent and intimidating in their treatment of African-American civil rights protesters. However, the

Supreme Court invoked the First Amendment to rule that public officials had to meet tough new tests before they could succeed in a defamation action, even if the allegations were proven false. This triggered a long line of cases in which US defamation law departed from British law, allowing for much more vigorous public criticism and debate.

The Electronic Frontier Foundation's 'Legal Guide for Bloggers' is targeted primarily at publication in the US, and sets out the elements of defamation as follows:

> a publication to one other than the person defamed;
> a false statement of fact;
> that is understood as
> a. being of and concerning the plaintiff; and
> b. tending to harm the reputation of plaintiff.
> If the plaintiff is a public figure, he or she must also prove actual malice.[22]

US law distinguishes between various kinds of plaintiffs including 'public figures' (those who court media attention), 'limited purpose public figures' (those in the public spotlight for a particular issue) and 'private figures'. Private figures do not need to prove actual malice on the part of the publisher, but need to show the publisher was at least negligent in publishing the defamatory falsity.

The two important differences between US and British–Commonwealth law are that in the US plaintiffs need to prove falsity, and if they are public figures they must also prove the publication was malicious. These differences mean you face much lower risk of libel action in the US over your blogging or social media messages on important public matters, but you need to be particularly careful if posting scandalous rumours about private citizens, especially if you know the allegations are untrue.

Europe

Article 10 of the European Convention on Human Rights protects free expression but states that it is qualified by 'the protection of the reputation or the rights of others'.[23] The nations of Europe handle this tension in different ways. The University of Oxford's Centre for Socio-Legal Studies produced an excellent comparison of defamation laws across twelve European jurisdictions showing the breadth of laws and approaches to damages and court costs.[24] Some nations follow the British law detailed above, and continental European countries typically offer plaintiffs a choice of criminal or civil libel actions and procedures. Some, like Belgium and Sweden, have strong constitutional protections for free expression above and beyond the European convention. Trial costs and damages are considerably higher in England and Wales than in other European jurisdictions.

Libel is sometimes punished as a crime with harsh penalties. In 2011, three Italian journalists were sentenced to jail and ordered to pay €12,000 in compensation to the mayor of Sulmona over corruption allegations. The sentence was criticised internationally as a breach of Article 10 of the European Convention on Human Rights.

A French case showed there could be other consequences of online defamation. Three French workers in a suburban Paris engineering company were fired in 2010 over their private Facebook postings criticising their workplace.[25] One complained about a boss and about being treated as a bad influence, saying he was 'part of a club of the unfortunates'; others responded with 'Welcome to the club'. The employment tribunal ruled that because their pages could be viewed by 'friends of friends', their defamatory remarks justified their dismissal.

Reputation damage in other regions

Most Asian countries have defamation laws in one form or another, which is not surprising given the shame attached to a 'loss of face' in many of these cultures. South Korean law has grappled with the advent of the Internet and has chosen to treat it like print, with both civil and criminal actions against defamation available.[26] Defamation can be punished there whether the material is true or false. In China, private citizens can push for prosecution of defamation under the criminal law, and the government can pursue charges if 'the state' or 'public order' has been dealt serious harm.[27] In late 2009, two Chinese bloggers were ordered to pay the equivalent of about US$40,000 in compensation to the widow of film director Xie Jin for claiming he died in the arms of a prostitute.[28] Japan offers both civil and criminal defamation options. Truth as a defence also carries a burden to prove an accompanying public interest in the material. Damages have traditionally been low.

There have been some interesting defamation actions in other parts of Asia. A Malaysian activist agreed to post an apology 100 times over three days on Twitter as part of a settlement following his allegation that a magazine company had treated a pregnant employee poorly.[29] He could not afford to apologise in newspaper advertisements. In Singapore, a former teacher won a lawsuit against a blogger who alleged she had been sacked for taking bribes to admit children to her school.[30] And in Vietnam, prominent gossip columnist Le Nguyen Huong Tra served three months in jail for alleging the son of a senior security official had affairs with beauty queens and dancers.[31]

Indonesia's *Electronic Information and Transaction Law Act* allows for up to six years in jail for criminal libel. Mother of two Prita Mulyasari was arrested under this law in 2010 after complaining on Internet mailing lists about the poor treatment she received at a private hospital. She was held for three weeks awaiting trial, but media coverage and a Facebook support site prompted her release on bail and she won her Supreme Court appeal against damages, only to be jailed under another provision.[32] Free speech groups are pressing for the law to be abolished.

African countries generally echo British or French defamation law, depending on their colonial origins. South Africa also has a criminal offence for the deliberate injury of another's dignity called 'crimen injuria'. In 2009 Duane Brady became the first South African arrested for this crime for posting a message about his wife's friend on Facebook.[33]

The laws in Latin and South American countries roughly follow their historical links with Spain and Portugal, while much of Caribbean law reflects its British heritage.

▶ Being liable for libel

It's no wonder defamation is a legal minefield for bloggers and other online writers. While the essential ingredients are similar the world over, there are major variations in the defences available and the constitutional frameworks underpinning them. This means trouble for Internet writers, because every online posting leaves you exposed everywhere your target has a reputation the instant it is downloaded there. That said, most western democratic nations offer generous defences on important matters of public interest that are reported fairly and accurately, particularly if you are just expressing a well-reasoned opinion about them. Blogging, Facebook statuses and tweets are all about expressing opinion, so if you stick to these basic principles you should be able to rest easy.

IN BRIEF: DEFAMATION

- Damaging someone's reputation online can trigger lawsuits and even fines and jail in some places.

- Someone can successfully sue for defamation if they are identifiable in your published work, even if you haven't named them.

- Blogs, tweets, Facebook entries, hyperlinks, emails and even retweets or 'Likes' might make you liable for defamation action.

- Ignorance is no defence, except for ISPs, which usually get immunity if they are unaware of defamatory material on their sites.

- Lawyers will advise you on defences you might be able to argue, such as truth, fair comment or privilege.

- Libellous material can sometimes be defended on the grounds that it is in the public interest.

- Defamation defences are strong in the US, especially if your target is a 'public figure'.

- No matter where you are, think twice before you blog about a person or company in a negative way.

- Defamation is a complicated field, so seek legal advice.

CHAPTER 3

SEE YOU IN COURT ...

Twitbrief: Take care with comments about courts and judges or you might become the defendant. #contempt #openjustice #injunctions #jurors #evidence

Let's hope you don't make the same mistake as Manchester mother of three Joanne Fraill, who was sentenced to eight months in jail by England's High Court in 2011 for exchanging Facebook messages with the accused in a drug trial while she was serving on the jury.[1] She also searched online for information about another defendant while she and the other jurors were still deliberating. All this went against the judge's clear instructions for jurors to stay away from the Internet.

As a blogger or social media user you might get to post your views blissfully for the rest of your life without ever needing to go near a courtroom. However, sometimes the justice system enters your world when you least expect it, with some major risks attached.

▶ Ancient rules for a wired generation

The first thing to understand about your relationship with the courts is that many of their rules were developed for an era when bewigged and robed judges slammed their wooden gavels on ornate mahogany benches as they berated the wretched accused, their snivelling counsel and the great unwashed in the public gallery. Reporters at the press desk dutifully took shorthand notes, then rushed to public telephones to phone through their stories to copytakers, who rushed the stories into newspapers before they went to press.

Parts of this scenario remain true today in some courts in some places, but they are at odds with the tide of technological and social change. Governments and judges are grappling with issues such as whether to allow audio or visual recordings of court proceedings, whether the media and citizens should be allowed to use social media in the courtroom and whether witnesses or jurors can Google the background of the accused.

Here we will look at the aspects of this fascinating topic that might directly affect you as a blogger or social media user: open justice, publishing restrictions, contempt of court and discovery.

▶ Tweeting from the courthouse

Times journalist Alexi Mostrous made the news with this tweet in December 2010: 'Judge just gave me explicit permission to tweet proceedings if it's quiet and doesn't disturb anything.' He was tweeting from WikiLeaks founder Julian Assange's bail hearing in London,[2] where chief magistrate Howard Riddle had granted reporters permission to post social media updates.[3] A few days later the High Court banned the use of Twitter in the appeal against that decision, later ruling it would be at the discretion of the judge in future cases.[4]

It was not actually a world first because other judges had allowed the use of Twitter in their courtrooms. Just over a year earlier, Australian Federal Court judge Dennis Cowdroy allowed technology reporters to tweet from his Sydney courtroom during the landmark iiNet copyright case.[5] Some judges in the US had already let reporters tweet from court, including Judge Mark Bennett in Iowa.[6] Others were much slower to embrace the practice.[7] New Jersey Centre County President Judge David E. Grine certainly did not tolerate this courtroom tweet by drink-driving defendant Scott Ruzal in May 2009: 'When all else fails, try ignorance. I watched four cops lie on a witness stand today and I didn't say a word.' His drink-driving and tweeting earned him a 33-day jail term.[8] German courts were also loath to allow the practice, with a reporter evicted from the District Court of Koblenz when he attempted to tweet from a murder trial.

Perhaps the first use of Twitter in a criminal justice situation was by student journalist James Karl Buck, who in April 2008 tweeted a single word—'Arrested'—on his way to the police station after being apprehended during an anti-government protest in Egypt.[9]

By mid-2011 social media was even being used by the police as a public-relations vehicle. In the UK, Birmingham police ran a 'tweet-a-thon' from a magistrate's court to show followers how their arrests worked their way through the system.[10] And in Australia, the Queensland Police Service allowed citizens to debate crimes, arrests and court appearances on its Facebook wall.

▶ Open justice in action

Each of these is an example of 'open justice' in action—a principle of public access to the courts entrenched in the legal systems of the UK, North America and Commonwealth countries through their connection with English common law, under which the judicial process has been relatively open since at least the twelfth century.[11]

It's not just countries of the former British Empire that have open courtrooms. Article 6 of the European Convention on Human Rights gives all citizens of that continent the right to a 'fair and public hearing',[12] while Article 11 of the Universal Declaration of Human Rights extends this to the rest of the world community with its guarantee of a 'public trial'.[13]

Under the principle of open justice, the judicial process should be transparent and open to public examination. Ordinary people should be able to sit in court and watch cases as they unfold. The media are seen as the 'eyes and ears' of citizens who cannot be in the courtroom to witness proceedings themselves. The extent to which all this applies to new media is still at issue as judges and magistrates ponder whether to allow reporters and ordinary citizens to blog or tweet from their courtrooms. Prominent Australian journalist Margaret Simons was threatened with contempt charges after tweeting reports from a Melbourne court without the magistrate's permission in 2011.[14] In Canada, an appeals court refused a teenager's request in 2011 for anonymity in a defamation action over online bullying on Facebook.[15] The court ruled that the open court principle was enshrined in the system and that defamation suits could not be conducted under a 'cloak of secrecy'.

Taken to its extreme, open justice can earn criticism for interfering with justice by tipping the balance towards 'trial by media'. High-profile trials in recent decades, such as those of O. J. Simpson and Michael Jackson, and the advent of programs such as *Judge Judy* have fuelled this concern. Somewhere in between is a happy medium where court processes are under examination but those accused of a crime can still get a fair trial.

▶ When courts affect bloggers and social media users

What kinds of situations can arise that might affect bloggers or social media users? Much will depend on the kind of blogger or social media user you are. If you are at the cyberjournalism end of the spectrum, the answer is obvious—you stand to deal with courts and the justice system in the same kinds of circumstances as reporters do, but perhaps without the same privileges granted to journalists. You might want to report or comment upon trials in your area of interest, but you might not have the privileged access to the courtroom and court papers or the protection of sources afforded to reporters in some places.

Perhaps your interest in blogging or social media is more as an activist or dissident. You might feel compelled to report or comment on court proceedings involving people fighting for the values or the principles you cherish. You could be like those who blogged and tweeted about the Julian Assange trial in London. Many had never been in a courtroom before and countless more chose to comment without attending the proceedings.

Perhaps you run a celebrity gossip site, blogging and tweeting about the court cases of the rich and famous. Or maybe you are a gardening or family history enthusiast and believe your posts are a world away from the courthouse. Think again: you don't have to be reporting on a case to find your writing affected by court decisions or your materials subpoenaed by a judge's order.

▶ Courting secrecy

Despite the existence of the open justice principle, online writers face restrictions on their reporting of crimes and other matters before the court. Your behaviour, postings and comments can lead to substantial fines or even jail terms. Reporters who cover court every day know the restrictions well and are trained to deal with them. As a blogger or other social media writer, your challenge is to brush up on what you can and cannot do.

The rules vary markedly between countries, but the most common constraints are on identifying victims of sex crimes (and sometimes those accused of sex crimes), juvenile offenders and witnesses, jurors and parties to family law disputes. Sometimes the whole court is closed for these proceedings or for other sensitive issues such as preliminary hearings, military and national security trials and mental illness matters.

The temptation for the gossip or sports blogger might be to mention these in postings about celebrities without being aware of the court restrictions on identification. Heavy fines and even jail terms apply in some places if you break these prohibitions. At the very least you need to check what bans apply in both your own jurisdiction and the place of the court proceedings before firing off those words or images.

▶ Gags, but not the funny kind

Sometimes judges will use their power to issue orders prohibiting publication of some aspect of a court case, or occasionally even the whole case. These are known as 'injunctions', 'suppression orders', 'gag orders' and 'stop writs'. When the orders ban you from revealing even the fact that the order has been issued, they are known as 'super injunctions'. These prompted a social media nightmare for the English courts when they were issued in relation to a number of privacy matters in 2010 and 2011. It came to a head in May 2011, when a football superstar was named in the House of Commons as the person at the centre of an anonymity injunction after tens of thousands of Twitter users had already tweeted his name.[16] A *Times* journalist was threatened with a contempt of court charge for tweeting the footballer's name to his followers in breach of the order.[17] It was believed to be the first time the Attorney-General had been formally asked to consider contempt charges against a social media user.

Gags like super injunctions have also been used in the US. The *New York Times* reported in 2008 that the owners of political website Room 8 received a grand jury subpoena to disclose the authors of some of their anonymous blogs.[18] They were threatened with prosecution if they revealed they had even received the subpoena. Legal blogger David Markus experienced similar frustrations after a judge in a terrorism trial issued a gag order and then partially lifted it in 2008.[19] Markus was then allowed to blog about some aspects of an ongoing immigration case on his Southern District of Florida Blog but not permitted to discuss details of an alleged bombing plot that shared many of the same facts.

Blogs covering sensitive national security information or sexual taboos are much more likely to be gagged, sometimes permanently. In 2007, Californian courts were able to uphold permanent injunctions against websites set up by a paedophile to track the movements of young girls at public events.[20]

▶ Take-down notices

Sometimes the injunction is in the form of a notice to take down certain material from a site or to shut down the whole site. This is sometimes issued to the ISP or search engine host. In 2011, Google complied with a 'preventative closure' order from an Italian court to remove the English-language blog Perugia Shock, which criticised aspects of the prosecution of an alleged murder of a British exchange student by her US room-mate. The blog reappeared elsewhere, the *Washington Post* reported.[21] In Australia, media organisations were ordered to remove material from their searchable archives that was related to the upcoming trial of a prominent criminal figure.[22]

▶ 'Held' in contempt—literally

Defiance of such a court order is just one form of contempt of court—a charge occasionally faced by journalists that can also take a blogger or social media user by surprise. According to *Nolo's Plain-English Law Dictionary*, contempt is 'behaviour in or out of court that violates a court order, or otherwise disrupts or shows disregard for the court'. The kinds of behaviour covered by contempt vary somewhat in different countries, and that is where you need to be careful.

First Amendment free expression rights in the US allow much more leeway than in other countries to publish material during a trial. Revealing jurors' identities and running commentaries on witness testimony are a regular part of the media circus in celebrity trials there. Many other countries restrict such coverage and commentary.

The first two areas of contempt below apply to the US; all five affect writers in many other parts of the world:

1. contempt in the face of the court (being rude or disrespectful in the courtroom)
2. disobedience contempt (disobeying a court order)
3. scandalising the court (publishing material claiming the judge is biased or has an improper motive)
4. *sub judice* contempt (publishing material that might prejudice a trial)
5. revealing juror deliberations (approaching, identifying or interviewing jurors).

We'll take a brief look at each of them to see where bloggers, social media users and journalists have run into trouble.

'The law is an ass—and so are you, Your Honour...'

'. . . with respect, of course.' Almost any behaviour that disrupts the courtroom can be considered a contempt of court. Over the years judges have charged people with 'contempt in the face of the court' for outright physical assaults in the courtroom, verbal abuse, inappropriate dress, sleeping, and even attempting to release laughing gas into the court building. In recent years people have been charged in India, the US and the UK over their phones ringing in court.[23] That's the most likely scenario for a blogger or social media user to be charged with contempt in the face of the court: if your device disrupts the court proceedings. Keep your phone turned off during trials, or at least have it switched to silent mode. And don't attempt to take any photos or make recordings in the courtroom unless you have been given specific permission to do so.

'Court order—so what?'

There are numerous examples of bloggers being jailed for defying court orders related to their writing and publishing. Disobedience contempt is the refusal to comply with a court order. While journalists have sometimes been jailed for refusing to reveal their confidential sources on ethical grounds, bloggers and website hosts have sometimes been imprisoned for other reasons. Some have an emotionally charged attachment to an issue behind their obstinate refusal to comply with a court order. Senior citizen Paul Trummel served almost four months in jail for contempt in Washington in 2002 when he refused to remove contact details of the administrators of his low-income residence from his website in compliance with a court order.

A Florida judge issued a warrant for the arrest of Kristen Rhoad on a civil contempt charge in 2006 after she ignored an injunction to remove all blog posts referring to her ex-husband, who had accused her of cyberstalking him. The Citizen Media Law Project reported that she removed the material as a result and the blog was no longer active.[24]

Ohio woman Elsebeth Baumgartner lost a defamation suit and then allegedly used her website to harass and defame the judge who had presided over the case. When he sued her over this behaviour, she then objected to the judge assigned to hear the case and insisted she recuse herself from the trial. Baumgartner was sentenced to 120 days' jail in 2006 on twenty-seven charges of contempt and fined US$2700. In 2010 the US District Court upheld her contempt conviction and sentence.[25]

A family dispute with her brother over the care of her elderly mother earned 59-year-old Michigan woman Diane Anderson a few hours in a high-rise jail with a picturesque view of the Detroit River for her behaviour in court and for comments critical of the judge made on her website, the First Amendment Center reported in 2008. She was released when Wayne County Probate Judge David Szymanski said he was wrong to have jailed her and then lifted his ban on her posting to her blog about the case, even though he knew there were 'lies' on the website.

And controversial Melbourne radio talkback host Derryn Hinch was sentenced to home detention in 2011 for naming sex offenders on his website and at a public rally.[26] This breached a court order suppressing their identities. Hinch had already served twelve days in jail in 1987 for broadcasting prejudicial material about sex offender Michael Glennon on the eve of his trial.

Reporters also sometimes refuse to comply with a court order to reveal their confidential sources. We will take a closer look at the issue of protecting sources in Chapter 6 when we consider the way confidentiality affects bloggers and social media users. Sadly, in many places you do not get to take advantage of the shield laws offered to mainstream journalists when trying to protect confidential sources in the courtroom.

Seeing scandals that aren't there

Conspiracy theories abound on the Internet, but they can get you into trouble in some countries under the rule of contempt by 'scandalising the court'. This involves effectively defaming the judge and the justice process in one fell swoop. For example, in 2003 a New Zealand-based website listed fourteen judges it was purportedly investigating for 'corruption, incompetence and suspect character', and threatened to release further information proving these allegations. This prompted a letter from the Solicitor-General and the material was subsequently removed from the site.[27]

Judges or magistrates might sue you for defamation if you write something nasty about them, but in Commonwealth countries the state might press a scandalising charge against you, particularly if you are claiming a judge was swayed by some outside pressure or improper influence in reaching a decision.

Sub judice—time to brush up on your Latin

The most frustrating area of contempt law for the traditional media has been *sub judice* contempt—publishing prejudicial material that might reduce the chance of a fair trial. First Amendment rights in the US have given the media immunity in recent times, but 'trial by media' can prompt a mistrial and lawyers can be disciplined if they make prejudicial statements during a trial. *'Sub judice'* is a Latin term meaning 'under justice' and has been prosecuted most often in the UK and Commonwealth countries, although some European countries, such as Denmark, have laws against publications that might seriously damage a trial.[28]

In 2011, the judge presiding over the trial of a conservative politician for a false expenses claim in Britain referred a potentially prejudicial tweet about the case by a rival politician to the Attorney-General.[29] High-profile Labour peer Lord Sugar tweeted to his 300,000 followers on the second day of the trial: 'Lord Taylor, Tory Peer in court on expenses fiddle. Wonder if he will get off in comparison to Labour MPs who were sent to jail?' The *Telegraph* quoted Justice Saunders as saying:

> I was concerned that if seen by a juror it might influence their approach to the case. . . I reported the matter to the Attorney-General not for the purpose of taking any action against Lord Sugar but to investigate whether entries on Twitter sites . . . posed a risk of prejudicing the fairness of a trial, and if so whether there were steps which could be taken to minimise that risk.

International media law firm Taylor Wessing defended a website against contempt allegations over prejudicial user-generated posts on a message board in 2009, just a few weeks before a criminal fraud trial.[30] The website was forced to take down the messages and the jury had to be warned not to do Internet research. Remember, as bloggers and social media users you are liable for your publications even when you do not intend to damage a trial. From the moment someone has been arrested in a criminal case, reports about the matter are seriously limited in many countries. Authorities can prosecute for this kind of contempt if there is a 'substantial risk' that justice will be prejudiced in the case.

While the mainstream media are the most common targets of such actions, the size of the audience for many blogs and social media commentators will increasingly make them vulnerable. The Victorian Government Solicitor's Office advises websites to take down materials related to an upcoming case in the lead-up to a trial.[31] The most sensitive material is anything implying the guilt or innocence of the accused, including confessions, photo identification of the accused and republishing reports of earlier hearings. A public interest defence might be available for publication of material on a matter of overwhelming public importance, but you should never rely upon this defence without legal advice.

Twelve Angry Jurors...

The film and Broadway play *Twelve Angry Men* depicted the intrigue and conflict of the jury room in a homicide case as jurors struggled to reach a verdict. The inside story on jury deliberations makes for fascinating reading, but such coverage is banned in many parts of the world.

Of course, the US has more freedom to name and interview jurors. In 2007 the Pennsylvania Supreme Court ruled that the disclosure of jurors' names gave the defendant a greater chance of a fair trial and demonstrated the fairness of the process to the broader community.[32]

There is also the issue of bloggers or social media writers becoming jurors themselves and then facing the temptation to tweet, blog or post Facebook messages from the courtroom during the trial. We started this chapter with the example of the British juror jailed for eight months for 'friending' the accused on Facebook and chatting with her. This kind of jury behaviour is broadly banned, even in the US. Retired Judge Dennis Sweeney spoke in 2010 about one of his own trials where five of the jurors 'friended' each other on Facebook despite his directions to avoid discussing the matter with anyone, particularly on social media.[33] Judge Sweeney also gave several examples of jurors misusing new media during trials, behaviour that led to mistrials and dismissal of jurors. He mentioned one Arkansas juror who tweeted from a trial in February 2009. One of his tweets could still be viewed online in late 2011.[34] Californian attorney Frank Russell Wilson was suspended from the bar for forty-five days for blogging about a burglary trial while serving as a juror. He had also failed to disclose to the court that he was a lawyer.[35]

A Sydney juror was charged with contempt in 2011 when she used a mobile phone in court to take a photo of a family friend who was sitting in a jury panel, as the *Newcastle Herald* reported. She was fingerprinted and her phone was seized. She was granted bail and the charge was later dropped, but signs were erected in the courthouse warning that no photography was allowed.

Jurors are now routinely given warnings about their use of technology and social media once they have been empanelled. Some US examples from state and federal courts are listed at goingpaperlessblog.com/social-media-in-the-legal-profession. But with so many citizens reluctant to even serve on juries it is hard to imagine many going 'cold turkey' on their social media use during a trial, particularly on those extending over weeks or months.

▶ Blogs, tweets and Facebook walls as evidence

'Anything you say or do can and will be held against you.' The 'Miranda warning' read by US police to suspects on their arrest also stands as good advice to bloggers and microbloggers. Every posting you make leaves a cyber-fingerprint that might be used in a courtroom as evidence of your views or behaviour. You might be subpoenaed for a case directly related to your publication—perhaps a libel action—or for evidence of a copyright breach. Or your blog, tweet or Facebook post might just contain something that sheds light on your behaviour or something about the life of someone you have written about or photographed.

Again, courts throughout the world have differing powers and procedures when it comes to gaining access to your accounts and publishing records in the pre-trial discovery process.

Despite First Amendment protections, US courts have often upheld subpoenas against bloggers, ISPs, search engines and social media enterprises such as Facebook and Twitter. Community news blogger Waldo Jaquith got caught up in the middle of a chicken farmer's lawsuit against local media in Virginia in late 2008. He was subpoenaed to provide all information he had used to write about the matter on his cvillenews.com blog, along with the identity and IP addresses of everyone who viewed the article and commented on it. By May 2009 the suit had been dropped, so Jaquith did not have to comply, but he wrote that he regretted not being able to set a precedent that bloggers would receive the same protection for sources that journalists do in Virginia.[36]

Fifty-three-year-old Texan Lyndal Harrington wrote for a blog on celebrity trials, www.rosespeaks.com, and as a result of her posts she was sued for defamation by the mother of the late model and actress Anna Nicole Smith. When the court subpoenaed her computer as evidence, Harrington claimed that it had been stolen from her house. The judge accepted the police account that the robbery had been staged and jailed Harrington for four days for contempt of court.[37]

In other countries First Amendment protections do not apply, so courts are even more willing to demand evidence from Internet writers related to the material they have posted. The one exception is defamation law, where judges in many Commonwealth countries are reluctant to order journalists to hand over materials or reveal their sources to litigants in the early stages of a trial, particularly if they appear to be merely fishing for the real culprit or a whistleblower in their organisation. This judicial discretion has been called the 'newspaper rule', but it might be due for a twenty-first-century name change.

▶ **'You are ... virtually ... served!'**

Some court practices have started to change with the times. Not that long ago you had to be served personally with a summons for a criminal charge or a writ for the launch of a civil action against you. A police officer or court official would knock on your door or approach you in public and say 'You are served!' as they handed you the formal document. In many places this can now be done online—via email or even via a message to your social media account. In 2008, the Supreme Court of the Australian Capital Territory became one of the world's first courts to allow legal documents to be served on defendants via private message to their Facebook accounts when they had defaulted on their home loan payments.[38] Other methods of contacting them had failed and their houses were about to be taken from them.

IN BRIEF: COURTS, JUDGES AND JURIES

- Judges can be fussy over protocols. Don't assume you can use electronic devices in court. Always check whether this is permitted.

- Open justice is a key international principle that implies the courts should be subject to coverage and critique.

- Judges have special powers to gag publications, including your blogs and social media postings.

- If you defy a court order you risk fines and even imprisonment.

- Judges can charge you with contempt of court over your behaviour in court, disobeying a court order, 'scandalising' the court, prejudicing a trial or breaking the rules applying to juries.

- If you ever find yourself on a jury, chances are you will not be able to blog or tweet about your deliberations.

- Lawyers will happily search through your blogs and social media postings if you are involved in a case to try to find prejudicial material about you.

CHAPTER 4

IDENTITY, ANONYMITY AND DECEPTION

Twitbrief: Pros and cons of fake identities. How well is your anonymity protected? #pseudonyms #hacktivists #disclosure

Identity and anonymity are moveable feasts in social media and the blogosphere. You might be comfortable blogging from behind a pen-name or Twitter 'handle'—yet be frustrated that you're not sure exactly who you are dealing with. Do you remember the case of that gay girl from Damascus? In the midst of civil upheaval in Syria in mid-2011, the world was concerned for the safety of lesbian Amina Arraf, who had been blogging for several weeks at A Gay Girl In Damascus. The international media, including well-respected outlets such as the *Guardian* and CNN, were following her fate, particularly after her 'cousin' posted a note to the blog saying Amina had been kidnapped by three armed men.

Suspicions about her identity were aroused when the *Guardian* ran a photo of the missing Arraf, which was soon identified as an image lifted from the Facebook page of London woman Jelena Lecic. As it turned out, 'Amina Arraf' was really forty-year-old American Tom MacMaster, a student at the University of Edinburgh. He outed himself and apologised for his four-month trail of deception.[1] The *Guardian* later published an explanation of how the organisation had been duped.[2]

Further enquiries by the *Washington Post* revealed Arraf's earliest posts had been to the Lez Get Real website. That site's gay editor, 'Paula Brooks', was revealed to be a retired military officer by the name of Bill Graber, posting under his wife's name.[3] He had even flirted online with MacMaster's character in bizarre exchanges where each thought the other was a lesbian.

But it didn't even end there. MacMaster was accused of adopting yet another persona to defend his role in the episode. The *Guardian* reported that a comment on the website Mondoweiss under the name 'Miriam Umm Ibni' had actually come from the same IP address in Edinburgh used by MacMaster for the Amina hoax.[4] When challenged, he said a female houseguest must have written it while visiting him.

It was an extremely tangled web of identity deception, complicated further by genuine concerns for the safety of homosexual women in Islamic states.

Less than a month later, in an extreme example of identity disguise, hackers broke into the @FoxNewsPolitics Twitter account and posted several false tweets claiming US President Barack Obama had been assassinated.[5] The cyberattack prompted a Secret Service investigation, but the irony was that Fox News' owner, News International, was in the midst of defending its own behaviour across the Atlantic, where reporters from the *News of the World* had spent years hacking the private phones and computer data of celebrities, politicians, police and other citizens. Then, just as owner Rupert Murdoch prepared to testify at a British inquiry into that privacy scandal, anonymous hackers from the group LulzSec broke into the website of his tabloid paper the *Sun* and posted false reports of the media mogul's death.[6] The series of events showed the bewildering interplay of identity, anonymity, security and deception in the online world.

▶ Sometimes it's hard to be me

It is not easy to decide whether to use your real-life identity or that of an alter ego when you are blogging or using social media. Either way, there can be legal consequences.

There are many sound reasons you might choose to use a pseudonym or 'handle' for your blogging and social media activities:

- It allows you to contribute to public debate while reducing the risk of verbal or physical attacks by people or governments who disagree with your opinions.
- It helps distance your personal views from those of your employer or your professional role.
- It lets you engage with others without the 'baggage' of your real life interfering with your message.
- It can be fun being someone else or even many other people!

Before you can be prosecuted or sued you need to be identifiable as a legal entity: a person or a corporation. Yet even if you operate under a pseudonym—which millions of bloggers and tweeters do—you are likely to be much more identifiable than you might first have thought. ISPs and social media enterprises like Twitter and Facebook have been ordered to reveal the identities of their anonymous clients in numerous court actions. Internet security experts and hackers suggest you reduce the risk of detection by setting up anonymous email and Twitter accounts and using Internet cafés for correspondence. There are many other safeguards for the online writer wanting to avoid detection, including using email address auto-destruct software, hiding IP addresses and disabling location tracking on smartphones when using social media.[7]

Such strategies may be essential for the dissident blogger operating in a highly censored regime. But if you're an anonymous writer in a country with a higher level of free expression, you might be tempted to operate with a dangerous level of bravado or spite because you think you will never be detected. Sadly, that belief has proven to be misguided in scores of cases throughout the world.

A useful guideline is that you should never publish under your pen-name anything you would not be prepared to take responsibility for if you were 'outed' at some later stage. Using a pseudonym might also lose you some of the legal protections your real name might earn you. For example, it might be hard to prove the opinion of your online persona was one you honestly held in real life, an element of a defamation defence in many places. Or your real-life identity might qualify you to protect your sources under a local shield law—particularly if you are a journalist—while your alias might not earn this privilege.

▶ @RussianPresident

There are also legal dangers attached to adopting someone else's identity in the form of a 'spoof' social media account or satirical blog. British businessman Mathew Firsht was offended when he discovered a former school friend had created a fake Facebook profile about him with very private information and untrue suggestions about his sexual preferences. The High Court of Justice awarded him £22,000 in damages for defamation and breach of privacy in 2008.[8] Fake pages can also infringe people's 'moral rights' under copyright laws, which we consider in more detail in Chapter 8.

Social media providers will shut down mischievous accounts set up using false identities, particularly if they pretend to be real people. The Twitter Rules explain that accounts can be suspended for a range of reasons, including impersonation: 'You may not impersonate others through the Twitter service in a manner that does or is intended to mislead, confuse, or deceive others.'[9] In July 2011, Twitter shut down the fake account @blog_medvedev established under the name of Russian president Dmitry Medvedev, a year after he had launched his official @KremlinRussia_E account and just weeks after he started his private account @MedvedevRussia.[10]

Facebook has a Statement of Rights and Responsibilities that requires users to agree: 'You will not provide any false personal information on Facebook, or create an account for anyone other than yourself without permission.'[11] It explains its procedures for reporting an imposter:

> If someone has created an account to impersonate or imitate you, please go to the impostor profile

and click 'Report this Person' in the left column. Check the 'Report this Person' box, choose 'Fake Account' as the reason, and add 'Impersonating me or someone else' as the report type. Be sure to add a valid web address (URL) leading to the real profile so that we can review the information.[12]

Despite their rules, neither Facebook nor Twitter are quick to suspend accounts that have not triggered complaints and are obviously satirical.

Operating a fake social media account or website for satire is one thing, but doing it mischievously is quite another, and most countries have laws forbidding such practices. In Texas, for example, a 2009 online harassment law was passed 146 votes to zero authorising judges to jail offenders for up to a year if they adopt another person's identity on social media to 'harm, defraud, intimidate or threaten'. But, as a local paper reported,[13] the law has been rarely enforced and Arlington Mayor Robert Cluck found it did not stop a satirical Twitter account using his name and photo.[14]

The false identities of others can be a trap, too. In mid-2011, thousands of Facebook users 'Liked' a PBS NewsHour story that rapper Tupac Shakur, shot dead in 1996, had been found alive and well in a small resort in New Zealand.[15] The sham story was the work of LulzSec hackers protesting a recent PBS documentary about WikiLeaks. Lesson: if it sounds too remarkable to be true, it probably is, so check it out further before sending it on. This comes back to the basic journalistic principle of verification—checking rumours out—a skill rapidly disappearing from the mainstream media and a rarity in the fast-paced world of social media.

▶ Hosting the words of others

Beware so-called 'user-generated content' on your blog, corporate website or even Facebook page. Courts and legislators are still uncertain on how to handle nasty anonymous comments on other people's pages. The liability of website hosts for the comments of others varies somewhat, so you would be wise to check on the situation in your home jurisdiction. As we have already seen, ISPs are immune in most places from actions over material published without their knowledge on sites they host, but they will normally be required to take offensive or illegal material down once it has been brought to their attention. In the US, section 230 of the *Communications Decency Act* gives immunity to anyone hosting the comments of third parties. It states clearly: 'No provider or user of an interactive computer service shall be treated as the publisher or speaker of any information provided by another information content provider.'

In 2011 the Federal Court of Australia found that a health company was responsible for fans' Facebook and Twitter comments on its accounts. These comments breached a court order that the company refrain from making misleading claims about its allergy treatments. The court ruled that the company should have taken steps to remove the comments as soon as it had become aware of them.[16]

Some countries take the liability of hosts even further. An anonymous political comment on Bashar Al-Sayegh's website landed the Kuwaiti journalist in jail for three days in 2007.[17] He was charged with insulting the Emir of Kuwait and only released from custody when authorities were able to locate the anonymous commenter.

As the host of your own blog or website, the question is whether you should allow an 'open comments' forum or instead filter each comment before approving its publication. While such screening might be time-consuming and might offend free expression and 'marketplace of ideas' principles, you will limit your exposure if you check each reader's response carefully before posting it. Alternatively, you might ask readers to post shorter comments via tweets mentioning your blog and Twitter handle. This will then make readers' comments their own publications rather than yours and give your blog wider circulation.

US citizens should also bear in mind the fact that most other nations do not offer immunity to site hosts for the comments of others. You should consider that you might be exposing the foreign site host to serious consequences if you vent your spleen in their comments section.

▶ **Deception in the public interest?**

Sometimes bloggers will use the age-old journalistic excuse for deception—that it was in the public interest. That was the argument Cuban exile Luis Dominguez gave for adopting the guise of a 27-year-old female Colombian sports journalist to trick Fidel Castro's son into sharing details of his opulent lifestyle. As the BBC reported, the blogger posted images and documents gathered through his online flirting with forty-year-old Antonio, who had a penchant for both sports and women.[18]

'I'm a Cuban and I'm a Cuban American and I have not been able to go back to my country since 1971 when

I left,' he told the BBC. 'I use whatever tools I have to be able to get back at these people. In Cuba people are put in prison for no reason at all. Their rights are violated . . . So, why can't I do the same thing to them? I have no remorse whatsoever.'

While public interest might be a worthy moral motivation for your deception, it will rarely work as a defence in its own right, particularly if your actions are criminal. Get sound legal advice before relying upon it.

▶ Marshalling an army of virtual people

Anonymity on the web is already being used as a marketing and PR weapon. The phenomenon of 'astroturfing' involves organisations' use of automated avatars to drown out the opposing views of real people on web forums. As the *Guardian* put it in an exposé in 2011, astroturfing is the use of 'fake grassroots campaigns that create the impression that large numbers of people are demanding or opposing particular policies'.[19] It revealed that even the US Air Force had called for tenders from companies to supply it with software that would create '10 personas per user, replete with background, history, supporting details, and cyber presences that are technically, culturally and geographically consistent'.[20] Just think—when you are dealing with the next gay girl from Damascus she might really be an avatar on a server in Florida. The practice is relatively new so the legal risks are still uncertain, but astroturfing could have implications in the areas of commercial and trade practices law if it involves misleading or deceptive conduct.

▶ Anonymity as a weapon for change

One group of so-called 'hacktivists' took anonymity to its extreme in 2003 and have since used the word 'Anonymous' as their name. They are responsible for a series of attacks against corporations, governments and organisations.[21] Most of their online assaults are in the name of Internet freedom and in retaliation against censorship practices. Anonymous is more a philosophy than a structured group, perhaps best described as a collective. But individuals throughout the world have been arrested for their alleged involvement in Anonymous. Many of these arrests followed Anonymous's attacks on major corporations such as Mastercard, PayPal and Postfinance in support of WikiLeaks in 2010 and 2011.

Australian man Matthew George, twenty-two, was fined A$550 for setting his computer to attack government websites in 2010 as part of an Anonymous campaign. He told the *Sydney Morning Herald* he was disillusioned by the experience: 'There is no way to hide on the Internet. No matter how hard you cover your tracks you can get caught. You're not invincible.'[22]

▶ Unmasking anonymous bloggers and social media users

The super-rich have gone to court in the UK and the US to try to find the identities of bloggers who have caused them grief from behind the shield of pseudonyms, but courts on opposite sides of the Atlantic have taken different approaches to this issue.

Legal case citations have traditionally used the names 'John Doe' or 'Jane Doe' for anonymous or confidential parties. (Some jurisdictions use 'Joe Bloggs'.) In May

2011, a Utah court ruled in favour of twenty-five John Does known as 'Youth for Climate Truth' who had set up a fake website and issued press releases claiming the powerful Koch Industries would stop funding climate change deniers.[23] The owners of Koch Industries, who were listed among America's top ten wealthiest people at the time, were angered by the spoof site and went to court to find out the identity of the protesters. But Judge Dale Kimball dismissed their motion for disclosure on the grounds that it did not meet the strict tests required to reveal the pranksters' identities.[24]

However, the High Court in England ruled in favour of another billionaire, Louis Bacon, who was attempting to force Wikipedia, the *Denver Post* and WordPress to reveal the identities of bloggers who had allegedly defamed him using pseudonyms. In late 2010, the High Court had also ordered the identification of another of Bacon's critics, who had created the website www.bahamascitizen.com. It seemed likely the US-based Wikipedia would protect its contributors' anonymity until it received an order from a US court with jurisdiction over its activities.[25]

Even in the US, authorities can move with considerable speed and secrecy to demand account details of suspects when plaintiffs or prosecutors can prove their action has merit. In 2010 the editor of the Home In Henderson blog, Jason Feingold, was ordered by the North Carolina Superior Court to turn over identifying information on six anonymous commenters on his blog post 'Arrest Made in Elder Abuse Case'.[26] The postings of 'Beautiful Dreamer', 'Fatboy' and others were ruled actionable and disclosure of their identities ordered despite

First Amendment and state shield law protections. Five of them later settled the defamation action.[27]

In mid-2011, Colorado District Court magistrate Judge Boyd N. Boland produced an excellent summary of US decisions on discovery of anonymous sources and pieced together the criteria US judges apply before ordering their identification in the course of delivering his judgment in *Faconnable USA Corporation v John Does 1–10*. The tough US tests pre-dated the Internet and were shaped by Supreme Court decisions over five decades protecting 'anonymous speech' as a First Amendment right. The landmark case was *Talley v California* in 1960, when the court ruled a city ordinance was void because it required all leaflets to contain the name and address of the person who prepared, distributed or sponsored it. Delivering the judgment, Justice Black stated an identification requirement would restrict free expression. 'Anonymous pamphlets, leaflets, brochures and even books have played an important role in the progress of mankind,' he declared. 'Persecuted groups and sects from time to time throughout history have been able to criticise oppressive practices and laws either anonymously or not at all.'[28]

In his *Faconnable* decision, Judge Boland cited *Talley* and explained that litigants seeking to 'out' an anonymous writer must:

- give notice of their action;
- identify the exact statements that constitute allegedly actionable speech;
- establish a *prima facie* ('at first sight') case against the defendant with enough evidence for each basic element of the action;

- balance the defendant's First Amendment right of anonymous free speech against the strength of the case;
- show that the disclosure serves a substantial governmental interest;
- ensure it is narrowly tailored to serve that interest without unnecessarily interfering with First Amendment freedoms; and
- convince the court that the case could not proceed without disclosure of the identity.[29]

Judge Boland was ruling on an attempt by high-end tailor and fashion retailer Faconnable to force an ISP to reveal the identities of John Does who had posted entries on its Wikipedia pages claiming the company was a supporter of Hezbollah, a Shiite Islamist militia and political party. Faconnable wanted to sue the John Does for trade libel and commercial disparagement, but was unsuccessful.

In early 2011, federal prosecutors had convinced a federal judge in Virginia to order Twitter to release the account information of Julian Assange and other WikiLeaks leaders as part of a grand jury probe into alleged criminal action. The judge rejected constitutional free expression and privacy arguments by Twitter, the Electronic Frontier Foundation and the American Civil Liberties Union that the details should remain confidential.[30] But the whole process had been kept secret until the judge 'unsealed' documents revealing the earlier stages of the prosecution processes. In late 2011, the appeal against the order was dismissed in the District Court.[31] The judge issued a 2703(d) order, allowing authorities to access materials from an Internet provider or website host 'relevant and material to an ongoing criminal investigation'. The wide-ranging order requested all 'contact information', including 'connection records, or records of session times and durations', and 'records of user activity for any connections made to or from the account along with IP addresses and all records or correspondence related to the accounts'.

The decision followed a series of similar court orders that unmasked anonymous bloggers, tweeters and Facebook users in both criminal and civil actions. The New York Supreme Court had ordered Google to identify an anonymous blogger in a defamation 'fishing expedition' in 2009. As a result, the operator of the Skanks in NYC blog was unmasked on the petition of fashion model Liskula Cohen, who had been denigrated in five postings about her sexual behaviour and ability.[32]

As we discussed in the introduction, a British local government body—the South Tyneside Council—managed to get a Californian order forcing Twitter to reveal the identity of anonymous bloggers who had been making 'false and defamatory' allegations about its councillors so they could launch defamation actions. It was a surprising decision, given the strong First Amendment protections in the US, particularly for criticism of political figures. London's *Telegraph* claimed Twitter had relented and handed over the identifying details of the users behind the accounts named @fatcouncillor, @cllrdavidpotts, @councillorahmedkhan, @councillorkhan and @ahmed-khan01.[33] While Twitter had previously been considered among the most defensive of its users' identity protection, a spokesperson said the most the company could be expected to do was to give anonymous bloggers advance warning that their details would be released so they had the chance to launch an appeal.

Lawyers for a famous Welsh footballer were not as successful in discovering the anonymous tweeters who had revealed the celebrity sportsman's name in breach of a UK injunction issued to protect his privacy. They had gone to London's High Court and won an order that Twitter reveal the details, but the US microblogging company seemed to have disregarded it because they were not obliged to comply with court orders from outside their jurisdiction.

Despite recent successes in the US, the Citizen Media Law Project lists several cases where litigants failed to meet the tough test needed to discover the identity of anonymous online writers:

- In Pennsylvania, William McVicker lost in an attempt to subpoena Trib Total Media, publisher of the *South Hills Record* and YourSouthHills.com, for the identities behind seven screen names as part of an employment discrimination case.

- In New Jersey, the President of the Galaxy Towers Condominium Association, Slava Lerner, failed to obtain the identities of commenters who 'accused [him] of improprieties' from Michael Deluca, publisher of GalaxyFacts, a website forum used by Galaxy Towers condominium owners.

- In New York, an Orange County grand jury subpoenaed a local weekly newspaper, the *Chronicle*, for information about the identities of two anonymous posters to its website who had commented on the Chester district's school superintendent. A judge

quashed the subpoena in 2010 because the identities
were not crucial to the matter at hand.

- A Missouri court denied a motion to compel *The
Springfield News-Leader* to identify 'bornandraised-
here', a commenter on its website. It held the writer
had First Amendment protections despite agreeing to
the newspaper's privacy policy before commenting on
an upcoming civil case.[34]

Even some traditional news organisations have tried to
discover the identity of bloggers when defending their own
interests. News America, publisher of the *New York Post*,
sought a subpoena in California in 2005 to force Google
to reveal the identity of a blogger who had breached its
copyright by posting its entire Page Six column without
advertisements.[35]

▶ Duty to disclose in the UK

In deciding whether or not to reveal the identities of
anonymous parties, UK courts draw on a decision made
by the House of Lords more than two decades before
mainstream use of the Internet. The 1973 case of *Norwich
Pharmacal v Commissioners of Customs and Excise* centred
on a company seeking the identity of those importing goods
that infringed their patents.[36] The customs commissioners
were ordered to reveal the identities of the importers.
As law firm Gillhams explains: 'The House of Lords
found that where a third party had become involved in
unlawful conduct, they were under a duty to assist the
person suffering damage by giving them full information
and disclosing the identity of wrongdoers.'[37]

In contrast to the US, disclosure has become the starting point in Britain. The High Court of Justice applied the *Norwich Pharmacal* test in 2009 when it ordered Wikipedia to reveal the IP address of an anonymous party who had amended an article about a woman and her young child ('G and G') to include sensitive private information about them.[38] The judge suppressed their names on confidentiality grounds because he believed the entries were part of a blackmail threat against the mother. Even though Florida-based Wikimedia—the owner of Wikipedia—was located in a US jurisdiction, the UK court issued the disclosure order. Wikimedia complied, but insisted it was not legally bound to do so because it was in a different jurisdiction and it had immunity under section 230 of the *Communications Decency Act* as a third-party publisher of the comments of others.

However, disclosure is not automatic in the UK courts. In 2011, British woman Jane Clift failed in her attempt to get the High Court of Justice to order the editor of the *Daily Mail's* website to reveal the identities of two anonymous commenters on an article about her. The newspaper and the website had run a sympathetic article about her winning a defamation action after the Slough Borough Council had published her name on a Violent Persons Register for merely reporting that a drunk had damaged a city flowerbed.[39] However, when anonymous critical comments appeared at the base of the web article, she tried to find their authors so she could sue them too. But Mrs Justice Sharp ruled that Clift had failed to satisfy the *Norwich Pharmacal* test. She said any libel action was unlikely to succeed because readers would not have taken the remarks seriously—they would have

considered them mere 'pub talk'. She gave greater weight
to the privacy interests of the anonymous authors.[40]

▶ Different rules in the Commonwealth

Canadian judges apply a different four-point test in
deciding whether they will protect anonymous bloggers'
identities. Judges need to consider whether:

- the unknown alleged wrongdoer could have a reasonable expectation of anonymity in the circumstances;
- the litigant has established a *prima facie* case against
  the unknown alleged wrongdoer and is acting in good
  faith;
- the litigant has taken reasonable steps to identify the
  anonymous party and has been unable to do so; and
- the public interest in disclosure outweighs the interests
  of free expression and right to privacy of the anonymous authors.

The test was developed in Ontario in a case stemming
from comments made on the political message board
Freedominion.[41] Two John Does—'conscience' and
'HR-101'—described human rights activist and lawyer
Richard Warman as a sexual deviant and a Nazi in
several postings visible to the site's 9000 users. Justice
Blishen ordered the site owners to hand over details
identifying the John Does, including their email addresses,
IP addresses and personal information submitted when
they registered for the forum.

But the same test had a different result in *Morris v
Johnson*, a case with similarities to the South Tyneside
Council matter. In July 2011, the Ontario Superior Court
of Justice refused to order the unmasking of local bloggers

who had criticised the Aurora city mayor. The Canadian Civil Liberties Union intervened to help protect the bloggers on the grounds that a *prima facie* defamation case had not been established and their free expression rights would be compromised.[42]

An anonymous 'poison-penner' was not so fortunate in Western Australia. A blogger using the pseudonym 'witch' launched a series of attacks on a stockmarket forum about technology security company Datamotion Asia Pacific Ltd and its Perth-based chairman and managing director, Ronald Moir. A court ordered the forum host HotCopper to hand over the blogger's details. At first these could only be traced to an interstate escort service, but private investigation by the plaintiff's law firm eventually found the true author of the postings, who was then hit with a $30,000 defamation payout.[43]

Many such cases have involved legitimate criticism of major corporations or wealthy public figures, and there are strong First Amendment arguments that a blogger's anonymity should be protected. CyberSLAPP.org was set up in 2002 by several free expression organisations to highlight the use of court actions by powerful litigants to 'out' anonymous critics. As their site explains, the groups propose a legal standard for courts to follow in deciding whether to compel the identification of anonymous speakers. They demand suitable notice, an opportunity to be heard, and the right to have claims of wrongdoing detailed before requiring identification. The coalition also sets out 'best practices' for ISPs. They feature scores of case examples on their website for the information of defendants. Coalition members include the American Civil Liberties Union, the Center for

Democracy and Technology, the Electronic Frontier Foundation, the Electronic Privacy Information Center, and Public Citizen.

Of course, you might face much more serious consequences if you operate under your true identity in some countries. As we have already observed, ISPs and other hosts have sometimes been all too willing to hand over dissidents' details to litigants and governments.

▶ Even some journalists oppose anonymity for writers ...

Despite the defence of anonymity by free speech groups, and the clear need for anonymity in some situations, some argue the protections have gone too far. You would think journalists would defend confidentiality of sources, but in 2010 even *American Journalism Review* editor Rem Rieder launched a stinging criticism of major news groups for allowing anonymous commentators to post offensive remarks on their websites.[44] Rieder pointed to the irony that newspapers had for decades conducted rigorous identity checks on letter writers, but now allowed their websites to run rampant with outright character attacks by anonymous commentators. 'One good reason to end the practice of allowing unnamed comments is that it's flat-out wrong,' he wrote. 'Another is that it is causing headaches for news outlets, headaches they seriously don't need, and it will cause more in the future.'

Australia's national daily newspaper the *Australian*, long an advocate of protections for confidential sources,[45] controversially outed a government worker in 2010 who blogged anonymous political commentary as 'Grog's Gamut'.[46] The newspaper's Media editor claimed it was his duty to 'out' public servants like Greg Jericho, who he claimed pushed a party-political line via his blogs and tweets. In the wake of the controversy, Jericho continued to write his blog at grogsgamut.blogspot.com, although he added a real-life bio and the disclaimer: 'The views expressed on this blog are mine and mine alone and in no way reflect the views of the Government nor any Department, nor do they in anyway reflect the work undertaken by me in my capacity as an employee of the Australian Public Service.' (He later took down the disclaimer after leaving the public service.) In the UK, blogger 'Night Jack' even went to the High Court in an attempt to stop *The Times* disclosing his identity.[47] We will look more closely at that case in Chapter 6 on confidentiality.

▶ *Nom de plume* or *nom de guerre*?

How would you categorise the pseudonym you use? Is it just a handle of convenience used for Twitter because it is witty and concise? Or does it allow you to take on a more literary persona, in the spirit of great authors' use of *noms de plume* ('pen names')? Or is yours better classed as a *nom de guerre* ('name of war'), used as a cover for your attacks upon others, for either principled or unprincipled purposes? Most of us would sympathise if you were using your false name because you feared retribution from a highly repressive regime; perhaps even if you feared your comments might cost you your job in a western democracy. As Rob Jenkins put it in the *Chronicle of Higher Education*: 'Anonymity is morally defensible when its purpose is to protect one's career or livelihood, but it becomes a form of cowardice—and thus reprehensible—when used to provide cover for character assassination.'[48]

Most of us have far less sympathy for bloggers or social media users who use the veil of anonymity to engage in the sport of character assassination, taking every opportunity to vent their bile at the expense of others. And courts in most countries will not tolerate it, particularly if it involves criminality. As London-based lawyer Lucy Middleton explained: 'The Internet is not the "Wild West" that many suggest, and anonymous lawbreakers may post at their peril.'[49]

IN BRIEF: IDENTITY AND ANONYMITY

- There are both advantages and disadvantages to remaining anonymous when blogging or using social media.

- Be aware that others are doing the same thing. Always check someone's real identity thoroughly before relying on their information.

- Your anonymity can never be guaranteed, so don't publish anything under your pen-name that you would not be willing to defend in real life. You might just have to.

- Remember that website hosts, ISPs and social media operators such as Facebook and Twitter will act to take down fake accounts under their own rules if they receive complaints.

- While the US offers you strong immunity against action over the comments of others on your blogs or websites, you can be held legally responsible for other people's comments in other jurisdictions.

- Anonymous bloggers have often been unmasked by other bloggers, the courts and the media.

- The rules on protection of bloggers' and tweeters' identities vary markedly between countries.

CHAPTER 5

PRIVACY AND SECURITY

Twitbrief: Private rights in a public world: celebrity suits, data protection and digital fingerprints.
#privacy #data #surveillance #cyberstalking

Let's journey back in time to Paris in 1867, when gentlemen still duelled to the death over matters of pride. The practice was masterfully recorded by Alexandre Dumas in his novel *The Three Musketeers*. Dumas lived an extravagant lifestyle in an era when the stars of print were the equivalent of screen idols today. He was besotted with 32-year-old actress Adah Isaacs Menken—the Paris Hilton of her time. The lovebirds posed for some saucy photographs (she in her underwear and he without the compulsory gentleman's jacket) but the photographer then tried to trade on their celebrity by registering copyright in the images. Dumas felt aggrieved but, as James Q. Whitman explained in the *Yale Law Journal*, the court held that his property rights had not been infringed.[1] However, the judge decided Dumas did have a right in privacy that trumped any property right the photographer might have held. With that decision, privacy was born as a right in the legal world.

Fast-forward to 2011: a court in London acted to protect the privacy of an extra-marital love affair between two modern-day celebrities,[2] but their identities went viral on social media, rendering the court order embarrassingly ineffective. A former reality TV contestant told the *Sun* newspaper about her sexual liaison with an unnamed footballer in a 'kiss-and-tell' account. She had demanded tens of thousands of pounds from the sports superstar to keep the affair secret and set up meetings in hotel rooms so they could be photographed by paparazzi. He rushed to court and won an interim injunction banning publication of his identity or details of his relationship with her. But many thousands of Twitter users defied the order, as did the *New Sunday Herald* in Scotland from beyond the reach of the English court's jurisdiction. Despite this level of coverage, High Court Justice Eady extended the injunction on the grounds that the footballer's identity was not yet sufficiently in the 'public domain'. He said that while it was possible blackmail was at play, his main concern was in protecting the privacy of the footballer for the sake of his wife and children, in line with earlier European privacy decisions. Within days a British journalist was being threatened with a contempt of court action for using Twitter to reveal the name of a different footballer and his lover,[3] who had won a similar injunction to protect their identities after a different affair.[4]

▶ From duels to court battles

The examples from 1867 and 2011 are from different eras but revolve around the same basic questions: does our society allow us to establish a shield around our private lives? Will the courts allow us to pursue those who intrude? What risks are attached to revealing private information about ourselves and others?

Another big question relates to the fact that both examples involved celebrities of the day trying to shield their private lives from public scrutiny. They wanted to trade on their personalities, yet protect their private lives from the public's voracious appetite for gossip about them. It is an issue that has led to a spate of celebrity privacy suits in recent years, particularly in the UK and Europe.

It came to a head with the *News of the World* phone-hacking scandal, with journalists, private investigators and news executives facing criminal prosecution for hacking the phones and message banks of the rich and famous, and even ordinary people caught up in high-profile tragic events.

Blogs and social media seem just as obsessed with celebrities and gossip as the mainstream media, so we need to look carefully at the legal risks of prying into the private lives of the stars.

Privacy rights and protections are a fairly recent legal development. For centuries gentlemen in Europe—and later North America—settled personal embarrassments and insults using the strictly codified practice of the duel, well documented in the ebook *Best Served Cold—Studies in Revenge*, available at inter-disciplinary.net.[5] Even today the tribal laws of many indigenous peoples prescribe a physical punishment such as a beating or stoning for causing another to 'lose face' in a community—actions covered by both privacy and defamation laws in the developed world.

While French courts were developing privacy law in the 1860s, there was no notion of a formal 'right to privacy' in the English-speaking world. Laws in the US, Britain and its former colonies had evolved over centuries to protect the individual's space and reputation in several ways, including defamation, copyright, trespass, nuisance and confidentiality.

In 1888, Michigan Supreme Court Justice Thomas Cooley wrote of a 'right to be let alone'. Then, in a landmark *Harvard Law Review* article in December 1890, the great American attorney Samuel D. Warren and future Supreme Court Justice Louis D. Brandeis announced a new 'right to privacy' in an article by that very name.[6] Warren had been angered when a daily newspaper had published the guest list of a high society dinner party his family had hosted at his Boston mansion, which he saw as a gross invasion of his privacy. The right to privacy in the US therefore owes its existence to a wealthy lawyer who resented the media prying into his personal life.

In 1890, Warren and Brandeis wrote: 'The press is overstepping in every direction the obvious bounds of propriety and of decency. Gossip is no longer the resource of the idle and of the vicious, but has become a trade, which is pursued with industry as well as effrontery.' Their words mirror those of the critics of celebrity gossip mags and websites today, particularly in the wake of the *News of the World* scandal.

The Americans proceeded to develop their new right to privacy over the next century, but a certain document—the First Amendment to the US Constitution—limited its impact on the media in that country, rendering the citizen's right to privacy merely a shield against overly intrusive government interference.

US privacy law has generally been categorised into four types, each with strong public interest and free press defences:

- intrusion: trespass, secret surveillance and misrepresentation
- appropriation: misappropriating the names or likeness of someone else
- false light: highly offensive portrayal of someone in a false or reckless way (similar to defamation)
- public disclosure of embarrassing facts: revelation of intimate details about someone that should be off-limits to the broader public.[7]

The legal and cultural differences between the US and European approaches to privacy were summed up well by Bob Sullivan of msnbc.com in 2006: 'Europeans reserve their deepest distrust for corporations, while Americans are far more concerned about their government invading their privacy.'[8]

▶ High aims with patchy application

The legal right to privacy is recognised in nearly every national constitution and in most international human rights treaties. Privacy wins protection at the highest international levels. It is included in the Universal Declaration of Human Rights (Article 12), the International Covenant on Civil and Political Rights (Article 17), the European Convention on Human Rights (Article 8), the American Declaration of the Rights and Duties of Man (Article V) and the American Convention on Human Rights (Article

11). A right to privacy has been upheld in the European Court of Human Rights and the United Nations (UN) Human Rights Committee.

The International Covenant on Civil and Political Rights states at Article 17:

1. No-one shall be subjected to arbitrary and unlawful interference with his privacy, family, home or correspondence, nor to unlawful attacks on his honour and reputation.
2. Everyone has the right to protection of the law against such interference or attacks.

Privacy gained traction in the Organisation for Economic Co-operation and Development (OECD) Privacy Principles,[9] which have provided the platform for basic enforceable data-protection regulations internationally. In other words, most nations and regional governance bodies agree that personal data should not be misused by governments.

But the broader application of privacy regulation sometimes falls down, either in the letter or the practice of the law. China, for example, protects privacy via passing mentions in its Constitution and labour and health laws, but government demands upon ISPs for personal data about their users indicate little official respect for the notion.[10] Malaysia has no constitutional protection of privacy, a fact bemoaned by its bar association after images of a Selangor politician taken within her home circulated in 2009.[11]

PrivacyInternational.org features a comprehensive guide to international privacy resources, including individual country reports. Caslon Analytics have also produced a useful international comparison of privacy laws, with several Asian and Pacific nations featured.[12]

▶ Vie privée

Continental Europe features civilian systems of law with strong privacy protections under their law of 'delict' (similar to the common law of 'torts') where citizens can seek compensation for infringements of their personality rights. German law divides privacy into the 'intimate', the 'individual' and the 'private', as Arnold Vahrenwald explained in his 1994 paper 'Photographs and Privacy in Germany'.[13] In France, specific rights of personality are identified, including the 'right to confidentiality of correspondence', the 'right to privacy of domestic life' and the 'right to a person's name'.[14] Many countries have reinforced the law of delict with privacy clauses in their constitutions and offences in their criminal laws. The chief document enshrining this is the European Convention on Human Rights. In Germany and France citizens have rights over their own image, so they can sue if they simply don't like the way you have used their photograph. Some, such as the New Yorker's Adam Gopnick,[15] have suggested that European laws have gone too far. When then International Monetary Fund head Dominique Strauss-Kahn was arrested over an alleged sexual assault of a maid in a New York hotel, it was revealed that the French media had been too fearful of breaching privacy laws to report an alleged history of earlier indiscretions. The charges against Strauss-Kahn were later dropped.

▶ Celebrity suits

For several decades, the right to sue over breaches of privacy failed to take hold in the UK or other common law jurisdictions such as Australia and New Zealand. The public interest in free expression held sway. A major turning point came in Britain and Europe with the death of Princess Diana in Paris in 1997 after a car chase involving paparazzi. Court decisions since then have moved towards a right to privacy.

In 1998, the UK passed its *Human Rights Act*, which incorporated the European Convention on Human Rights into British law, including a right to privacy (Article 8) and a right to free expression (Article 10).[16] From that moment, the approach of the UK courts started to take on the flavour of their continental European neighbours, who had already developed a strong privacy tradition.

Many of the UK judges avoided the words 'right to privacy', preferring to bend and stretch the ancient action of 'breach of confidence' to suit privacy ends, but the outcomes were the same. Most of the cases in the UK and Europe involved litigants from the ranks of entertainment, sports and royalty. Notable cases included:

- Actors Michael Douglas and Catherine Zeta-Jones convincing the High Court in 2001 and on appeal in 2005 that *Hello!* magazine had breached their confidence and invaded their privacy by publishing unauthorised photographs of their wedding taken by a paparazzo posing as a guest.[17]
- The House of Lords ruling in 2004 that supermodel Naomi Campbell's confidence and privacy were betrayed by the *Mirror* newspaper when it printed a photo of her leaving a drug rehab clinic.[18]

- The European Court of Human Rights finding Princess Caroline of Monaco had a right to privacy in 2004 when she was photographed with a long lens while holidaying on a public beach.[19]
- Prince Charles winning an action in 2006 against the *Mail on Sunday*, which had published extracts from his private journals.[20]
- The royal editor of the *News of the World*, Clive Goodman, and private investigator Glenn Mulcaire being jailed in 2007 under phone-tapping laws for intercepting the mobile phone messages of Prince William, sparking an avalanche of other charges in ensuing years.[21]
- A Paris appeals court fining British paparazzo Jason Fraser and *France Dimanche* in 2008 for invasion of privacy over photos of the late Princess Diana kissing her then-boyfriend Dodi Fayed on a yacht.[22]
- Actors Hugh Grant and Liz Hurley and her then-husband, Arun Nayar, settling with two photo agencies and two newspapers for £58,000 over photos taken while they were on vacation in the Maldives.[23]
- Formula One boss Max Mosley being awarded £60,000 in 2008 for invasion of privacy over a *News of the World* story headed 'F1 boss in sick Nazi orgy with hookers', based on secret filming of a sadomasochism session.[24]
- *Harry Potter* author J.K. Rowling winning an appeal in 2008 to prevent further publication of images of her young son taken with a long-lens camera in a public place. The court ruled that children had a stronger claim to privacy than adults.[25]

This list is a who's who of the rich and famous, and while the decisions concerned the traditional media, the principles apply equally to bloggers and social media users: unlike in the US, courts in the UK and Europe will not tolerate salacious intrusion into the lives of very public figures.

The decisions were reinforced throughout 2010 and 2011, when the UK courts issued at least eighteen non-publication injunctions ordering that the identities of several high-profile people be kept secret when exposés of their private lives were about to be revealed in the media. Some of the matters, such as the celebrity footballer case profiled at the start of this chapter, involved elements of blackmail. Judges suspected that celebrities might be subjected to threats that their identities would be revealed to the tabloid press if they did not pay their secret lovers. Some fell into the category of 'super-injunctions'—where it was prohibited even to reveal that an injunction had been issued.

Not all of the injunctions concerned the rich and famous, and they were even extended to include social media users by a judge in mid-2011. The Court of Protection's Justice Baker banned Facebook and Twitter users from identifying a brain-damaged woman in a case where her mother was applying to withdraw her life support.[26] And Lord Judge, the Lord Chief Justice, warned Twitter users and bloggers that they would be prosecuted if they breached court orders.[27] However, any ban was restricted to the England and Wales jurisdiction. Wikipedia, based in San Francisco in the US, vowed it would allow this information on its site in breach of the UK court orders.

▶ Privacy rights in the Commonwealth

Mike and Marie Hosking were New Zealand media personalities who adopted twins. When they later separated, they asked for respect for their privacy, but a magazine photographer snapped Marie walking the twins in their stroller in a public place. They sued, claiming breach of privacy. The NZ Court of Appeal took the opportunity to introduce a new action for breach of privacy, but held that it did not apply in the Hoskings' case. The Kiwi test, as outlined by Justice Gault, sets out two fundamental requirements for a successful claim:

1. the existence of facts in respect of which there is a reasonable expectation of privacy
2. publicity given to those private facts that would be considered highly offensive to an objective reasonable person.[28]

There was still no common law right to privacy in Australia in 2012, although laws of data protection, trespass and breach of confidence went part of the way to protecting the privacy of citizens. The *News of the World* scandal in the UK prompted calls for a new privacy tort as had been recommended in 2008 by the Australian Law Reform Commission.[29] District and county court decisions in Queensland and Victoria proclaimed a new tort of privacy breach, but superior courts had not yet followed their lead. The High Court famously left the door open for a possible privacy tort in the *Lenah Game Meats* case in 2001, when animal liberationists had trespassed to film the slaughter of possums in an abattoir in Tasmania.[30]

▶ Data and dirty secrets

Privacy law is not just about celebrities suing tabloids over intrusion into their personal lives and relationships. A much larger area of privacy law is built around the storage and handling of your personal data by governments and corporations. If you host a site, it also controls the way you can manage information about other citizens, particularly if you are charging them for subscriptions or selling them services.

There are data-protection laws in most countries, typically restricting the use of your private details to a narrow set of circumstances related to that department's or organisation's business. They need your permission to use the private facts and then need to comply with regulations on their secure storage.

European Union countries have a particularly strict regime of protocols controlling the management of private data, both in digital and physical forms. It is known as the Data Protection Directive and applies to any identifying information about individuals.[31] It covers any person or company trading with EU countries, so it would apply to foreign blogs with EU clients.

You will often hear stories of the breach of data-protection laws, either in a physical or digital form. In 2005, blogger Elisa Cooper became the first individual targeted by the California Department of Managed Health Care after she posted a link to the private medical records of about 140 clients of the healthcare organisation where she had worked.[32] Her former employer—Kaiser Permanente Health Group—had inadvertently uploaded the material to its website. She was their former website designer and was so angry about their data-handling practices that she set up the blog, calling herself the 'Diva of the Disgruntled'. The company was fined US$200,000; it then launched an action against Cooper to force her to take down her blog.[33]

Private medical data goes public all too often. In North Carolina in June 2011, Fox8 reported that fifteen boxes of private medical documents were found in a home rented by a former medical centre employee.[34] State identity-theft legislation required the medical centre to report the documents as missing but they had not done so. Try a simple Google search for 'medical records found' and you will see how often private data goes missing.

But those incidents pale in comparison with Sony's massive data breach incident in 2011: the account information of almost 100 million of their PlayStation Network clients was hacked, placing at risk the security of more than 12 million credit cards.[35] Miller Thomson lawyers reported that at least fifty-eight class action lawsuits had been launched in the US and Canada as a result of the data breach, prompting further litigation between Sony and its insurers.[36] Clearly, poor data security can carry expensive legal risks.

Dallas woman Cathryn Harris and others filed a class action against Facebook and Blockbuster over an automated system called 'Facebook Beacon' which notified their friends on the social network every time they rented a video online from Blockbuster.[37] The two companies shared clients' personal information under their agreement, which Harris claimed was a 'civil conspiracy' to violate the *Video Privacy Protection Act*. A similar action was launched in California by Sean Lane, whose wife discovered via Facebook Beacon that he had bought her jewellery on overstock.com, spoiling her surprise gift. *Wired* reported that Facebook settled the actions in 2010 by agreeing to shut down Beacon and pay US$9.5 million into a Digital Trust Fund, with at least $6 million going to research into online privacy.[38]

The US Supreme Court decided in 2011 that the term 'personal privacy' applied only to 'natural persons' and not to corporations trying to avoid the release of sensitive internal data in answer to 'freedom of information' requests.[39]

If you are blogging or operating a website for a company or government department, you should study your country's data-protection and privacy regulations carefully. If you collect personal data on subscribers to your blog, you should first check this practice against local privacy laws—particularly if you intend onselling any of the information to other parties. Doing so without legal advice could place you in serious violation of privacy laws in many countries.

▶ Damn those digital fingerprints

While your online activities might expose you to the risk of privacy action, what about your own privacy when you operate as a publisher, blogger or microblogger? The sad reality is that we put our own privacy at great risk every day, both physically and digitally. Most of us don't follow the advice to shred private household documents before throwing them away. Nor do we destroy computer hard drives or smartphone SIM cards when we replace them. Such devices contain the basic ingredients for identity theft for any criminal who finds them. They can also contain incriminating evidence if you are travelling through countries with different standards of free expression or morality.

The large volumes of private information held on every UK citizen by governments and corporations was highlighted in the documentary *Erasing David*, in which a man went into hiding and hired some of Britain's top investigators to try to find him by discovering everything they could about him via public and private files. He found it was impossible for him to lead a private and anonymous existence in the UK in the twenty-first century.

Our digital trail extends wherever and whenever we conduct business on the Internet. The typical web browser stores countless 'cookies' that track our online activities. Search engines, app stores, airlines, travel booking agencies and scores of other online entities hold all sorts of digital information about us that may or may not be secure. It may even be subject to legal discovery (official demand for evidence) in the case of a court action. Some European experts are so concerned about the amount of irretrievable information about us out there that they are proposing a new 'right to be forgotten', allowing citizens to have their personal data permanently erased.[40]

Law-enforcement authorities throughout the world are winning court orders to search suspects' Internet records. Facebook is a popular hunting ground, with Reuters reporting that federal judges in the US had approved more than two dozen applications to retrieve incriminating data from Facebook accounts between 2008 and 2011, leading to several arrests and convictions.[41] The Electronic Frontier Foundation has published a useful online Know Your Rights! guide for US citizens faced with the threat of search and seizure of their devices by law-enforcement authorities.[42] EFF attorney Hanni Fakhoury has expressed concern at the volumes of private information the average citizen holds on their personal devices:

> With smart phones, tablet computers, and laptops, we carry around with us an unprecedented amount of sensitive personal information . . . That smart phone in your pocket right now could contain email from your doctor or your kid's teacher, not to mention detailed contact information for all of your friends and family members. Your laptop probably holds even more data—your Internet browsing history, family photo albums, and maybe even things like an electronic copy of your taxes or your employment agreement. This is sensitive data that's worth protecting from prying eyes.[43]

Sometimes, though, this stored data keeps killers off the streets. Messages to his mistress on a service called Kakao Talk were the undoing of a Korean computing professor who had strangled his wife and tried to dump her body in the Nakdong River.[44] He had even visited the social networking company's offices to get them to delete crucial text messages he had sent his mistress, but that data, combined with surveillance camera footage, formed the basis of the prosecution's murder case against him.

Of course, basic password selection and management is a fundamental starting point we often overlook. As the computer experts advise, choose your passwords carefully and change them often. Laptops and smartphones also have geolocation capability, meaning your very movements can be recorded and abused. This has serious implications for any meetings or communications you might have with confidential sources for your blog, an issue we examine more closely in the next chapter.

As the Pew Research Center reported in 2011, more than half of all people online had uploaded photos to be shared with others.[45] Now that facial recognition ('tagging') is increasingly combined with geolocation capabilities, we are leaving digital footprints via our images. That seems fine when you are just sharing an image with your small circle of friends on Facebook, but depending on your privacy settings, these photos might well be viewable to the outside world—and even if you have deliberately limited access to people within your immediate network, your 'friends' might choose to download and forward your photographs.

Do others have the right to use your images in their postings? And do you have the right to use their images? As far as privacy goes, the courts have given us very little guidance on this to date. (Intellectual property is a separate issue, and we'll look at it in Chapter 8.) If someone has their privacy settings on maximum restriction, or just emails a revealing image to a small circle of people, then re-sending or posting that image might be classified as a breach of confidence or the disclosure of embarrassing private facts. Hacking into someone's account to bypass their privacy settings can be a simple—but illegal—process, as a security expert learned when he demonstrated the procedure at an Australian conference and a journalist was detained and questioned after reporting on the technique.[46] In 2011, the US state of Tennessee passed a law making it an offence for anyone to post an image that causes 'emotional distress' to someone else, although its constitutionality has been questioned.[47]

Our decisions about whether to publish the images of others are not yet legal ones under the privacy laws of many countries. Instead they fall within the realm of moral or ethical judgments, and we all know how murky that area can be with so many different cultural, religious and ideological factors at play. Prevention is better than cure. The simplest approach is to avoid ever emailing or posting an image on the Internet if you would be unhappy for that same image to appear on that night's network news with your name attached to it.

▶ Cyberstalking and bullying

Another type of privacy breach takes the form of harassment. Things can get pretty heated out there in cyberspace, and most people know when to walk away from an online disagreement. But, just like in society generally, some personality types just won't let go and things can turn very nasty. Stalking laws in many countries extend to digital intimidation.

Sometimes there is a fine line between satire or parody and cyberbullying, particularly when the behaviour stems from relationships that have turned sour. Fake Facebook pages or Twitter accounts sometimes include false private details of the target's sex life or private affairs, triggering legal action. As we saw in Chapter 4, a UK court awarded damages for breach of privacy and libel in 2008 over a bogus Facebook page that falsely claimed a businessman was gay.[48] The case was interesting because it showed that even false private information could be considered a breach.

But two cases in the US showed the extent to which free expression protections applied to such satirical blogs in the States. In Texas in 2006, two Clark High School students set up a fake MySpace page in the name of their vice-principal, Anna Draker, including her name, image, details of her workplace and graphic sexual comments about her. She sued the students for defamation and their parents for negligence in not supervising their Internet use. She lost the defamation case on technical grounds. An appeal court judge said there was no effective remedy for 'intentional infliction of emotional distress' despite the students' behaviour being 'outrageous'.[49] A Californian court also found the First Amendment protected a satirical blogger who set up a fake blog to mimic and mock the blog run by her former friend. Christy Lochrie was a reporter for the *Record Searchlight* in Redding and penned a blog called 'Phat and Pink' on the paper's website. She had fallen out with her friend Beth Doolittle-Norby during their protest against a local bar's policy of banning overweight women. To spite her, Doolittle-Norby set up the fake blog 'No Phat Pink Chicks', making fun of Lochrie's writing, looks and personality. But the court denied Lochrie's attempt at getting a restraining order to stop Doolittle-Norby harassing her. While the fake blog was childish and nasty, it still earned free speech protection. 'We do have this animal called blogging and we're going to have to live with it,' the *Record Searchlight* quoted the judge saying.[50]

An Ohio woman even sued a blogger for trespass because his site prompted people to wander into her family's property looking for ghosts. Melissa Duer was the owner of an historic mill near Dayton. Andrew Henderson ran the Forgotten Ohio website which included a whole section on ghost towns. He claimed the mill was haunted.

She sued, claiming the site had portrayed her family in a false light, had intentionally caused emotional distress, and had triggered the trespasses on to her land. She was awarded a default judgment of US$129,794 because Henderson did not appear in court to defend himself, but she failed to prove the trespass element of the suit.[51]

Canadian courts seem to have adopted a position on such cases somewhere between the Europeans and the Americans. As we saw in Chapter 3, the Nova Scotia Court of Appeal refused a request by a teenage victim of cyberbullying that she be allowed to sue her bullies under a pseudonym so she would not be subjected to public humiliation. But the court would not allow her libel claim to proceed 'under a cloak of secrecy' after weighing her privacy against free expression and open justice interests. 'Should she be successful, one might expect that she will be lauded for her courage in defending her good name and rooting out on-line bullies who lurk in the bushes, behind a nameless IP address,' the judge declared.[52]

IN BRIEF: PRIVACY

- Research and comply with your own country's data-protection laws if you plan to collect or trade in personal information.

- Never breach a court order banning someone's identification.

- Blog, tweet and post about matters that are clearly in the public domain, not about people's private lives.

- Take special care and get legal advice if you plan on setting up a spoof site pretending to be another real person.

- If you have an anger-management issue or just can't let go of emotional baggage, see both a psychologist and a lawyer before you launch a campaign of cyber-revenge.

CHAPTER 6

CONFIDENTIALITY IN A MEDIUM WITH FEW SECRETS

Twitbrief: Secrets, breach of confidence and off-the-record sources for online writers. Plus, shield laws: do bloggers qualify? #confidentiality

'Psst! Wanna know a secret? Strictly off the record ...' Investigative journalists and political reporters have always been reliant on leaks from confidential sources and have developed protocols for dealing with them. In some parts of the world, legislators have helped out by introducing shield laws for journalists or publishers that help protect the identity of their sources if the leak becomes part of a court case.

But bloggers and social media users are a different story. Firstly, unless you are a former journalist you are unlikely to have training or experience in handling off-the-record information and covering your trail so your whistleblower is protected. Secondly, only some of the shield laws designed for journalists have been extended by legislators or the courts to apply to bloggers or microbloggers.

In this chapter we look at this issue of confidential information and the protection of sources, and narrow down the key points you need to consider before handling off-the-record information in your online research and writing.

▶ Strictly confidential ... for celebrities

There is no clear dividing line between confidentiality and the topics of anonymity and privacy we have already covered. It also overlaps with defamation, intellectual property, national security and freedom of information laws because these can all involve confidential information. We saw in the last chapter that some of the biggest celebrity privacy cases in the UK and Europe in recent years have involved at least some element of breach of confidence. The British courts have used the breach of confidence action as a way to meet the privacy requirements of the *Human Rights Act*, which married the European Convention on Human Rights with English law. As noted previously, that happened in 2001 when actors Michael Douglas and Catherine Zeta-Jones sued *Hello!* magazine for publishing photos of their wedding. They had signed an exclusive £1 million deal with *OK!* magazine for the coverage of the reception. The High Court held *Hello!* magazine had 'breached their confidence' by publishing images taken by a photographer who posed as a wedding guest. And the same principle was applied by the House of Lords in 2004 when it found the *Mirror* newspaper had breached the confidence of supermodel Naomi Campbell by publishing images of her leaving a Narcotics Anonymous clinic.

▶ Confidentiality in the US

In the US, there is a rarely used action of 'breach of confidence', usually employed against doctors who have disclosed a patient's identity. For example, an Oregon mother sued a doctor for breach of confidence when he helped identify her to a daughter she had given up for adoption at birth.[1] But most allegations of confidence breaches involve either privacy or trade secrets laws. Personal secrets are usually dealt with under the privacy laws, particularly the law of public disclosure of embarrassing private facts. The Florida Bar gives examples of such facts as sexual relations, family quarrels, humiliating illnesses, intimate letters, details of home life, private and stolen photographs and income tax return details.[2] There are strong public interest and First Amendment defences. The Citizen Media Law Project sets out the elements of this action:

- public disclosure: the disclosure of facts must be public
- private fact: the fact or facts disclosed must be private and not generally known
- offensive to a reasonable person: publication of the private facts must be offensive to a reasonable person
- not newsworthy: the facts disclosed must not be newsworthy or a matter of legitimate public concern.[3]

Commercial confidentiality in the US is covered by trade secrets law. The *Uniform Trade Secret Act* deals with commercial information that is secret, confers a competitive advantage on its owner and has been subject to reasonable efforts to maintain its secrecy.[4] It can cover business information such as customer or supplier lists, financial data, staff details, formulae, designs, patterns, plans, software, processes and other 'know-how'.

▶ Confidentiality in Europe

The law of confidentiality in most European countries is hard to distinguish from the privacy law detailed in the last chapter, although Article 8 of the European Convention on Human Rights also confers upon all citizens a right to respect for their correspondence. One of the French rights of personality is the 'right to confidentiality of correspondence' and this is also stated in legislation in Bulgaria and Estonia. The Global Internet Liberty Campaign lists several other confidentiality provisions throughout Europe,[5] including Switzerland's professional confidentiality protections for medical and legal information under its penal code and Latvia's rights to 'confidentiality of correspondence, telephone conversations, telegraph and other communications' under its constitution. Argentina and Brazil, with legal origins in Europe, also protect the confidentiality of correspondence in their constitutions.

▶ Confidentiality in the UK and Commonwealth

The law of breach of confidence also exists in the former British colonies under the common law, although most have not merged it with the right to privacy as the UK judges have done. Many of the breach of confidence actions brought in Australia, New Zealand and Canada have involved corporate secrets.

As the Vancouver-based McConchie Law Corporation explains,[6] anyone claiming a breach of confidence under common law needs to prove that:

- The information conveyed was confidential.
- It was communicated in confidence.
- It was misused by whoever received the communication.
- Its misuse was detrimental to the complainant.

The test was developed in the English Court of Appeal in 1948 and has been applied in numerous cases throughout the Commonwealth.

To qualify, the secret information must have a 'quality of confidence' about it—something in the nature of the information itself that makes it confidential. While merely stamping something 'confidential' does not make it so, it might give rise to a contractual obligation to treat it as if it is. Even if the information originally had a 'quality of confidence', it may have lost it by having been relayed to so many people that it is now in the 'public domain'. A British court ruled that this had happened in 2011 when the BBC failed to prevent driver Ben Collins from revealing in his autobiography that he had been the secret driver 'The Stig' in the popular television program *Top Gear*. The judge decided there had been so many press reports about the matter in the lead-up to the trial that the secret had now become part of the public domain and there was no longer a confidence to be protected.[7]

The circumstances in which the information was obtained must have given rise to an obligation of confidentiality. The courts will look to whether the person who received the information knew it was confidential—or darned well ought to have known it was. Sometimes, the nature of the material itself is enough to meet this test, such as information about a person's discussions with their doctor. There is no need for the owner of the secret to have used the words 'this is confidential' for it to qualify. The circumstances in which the information was disclosed, such as a job interview, can also be enough to give rise to the obligation of confidence. This principle also binds secondary recipients such as journalists or bloggers, who will be bound if they should be able to tell from the circumstances of their receipt of the information that it is confidential. For example, if you receive a private Direct Message on Twitter from a contact in WikiLeaks directing you to certain information, you would likely be on notice that it is confidential. Of course, no obligation arises if you already have the information or if you can easily get it from someone else.

Before a breach of confidence can be proved, a court would have to show that you have disclosed the information, or at least threatened to do so, to the detriment of the plaintiff. It's irrelevant whether you disclose the information accidentally—you are still liable. Any use other than an authorised use will constitute a breach of confidence.

Confidential information can include documents, ideas, words and objects. It is most commonly information of a sensitive financial, legal or private nature. In the *Lenah Game Meats* case, Australia's High Court said that even a photograph 'illegally or improperly or surreptitiously obtained, where what is depicted is private, may constitute confidential information'.[8] This casts the lifting of people's Facebook photos in a new light, particularly if you have worked your way there via friends of friends or have hacked your way through their privacy settings to get them.

The obligation of confidence can arise in a host of situations, including the terms of a contract (written or verbal); the employer–employee relationship and associated trade secrets; the professional–client relationship; the transfer of a secret to a third party if the third party knows (or should know) it is confidential; or under legislation that applies to government information, such as cabinet documents or tax files.

The obligation can also apply to unsolicited information, such as the bundle of documents that 'falls off the back of a truck' and into a blogger's inbox. The test is whether its nature, and/or the circumstances in which it was received, suggest an obligation of confidence.

If someone has their privacy settings on maximum restriction, or just emails a revealing image to a small circle of people, then re-sending or posting that image might be classified as a breach of confidence or the disclosure of embarrassing private facts.

▶ Governments faced with tougher test

If the information relates to government or its operations, there is an extra requirement that needs to be met before a breach of confidence can be established. It must be shown that its disclosure would be contrary to the public interest. This applies to information about government and its workings, including information on national security issues, foreign affairs or information that would prejudice the ordinary operations of government. It does not apply to confidential information the government may hold that relates to private individuals or companies. There, the standard three-point test applies.

▶ Defending your blabbing

The best defences to almost all the confidentiality-related actions in the US are on First Amendment, newsworthiness or public interest grounds, as detailed by the Citizen Media Law Project.[9] The grey area here is whether bloggers, tweeters and other social media users qualify for the same First Amendment and newsworthiness protections as mainstream journalists. Much of this will depend on what they are publishing and whether it is seen as a gratuitous betrayal of a secret or the revelation of material of genuine public concern and importance.

In Commonwealth jurisdictions the law provides some limited defences to breaches of confidence, the most straightforward being that you were ordered by a court to disclose the confidential information. This might not suit journalists or bloggers who feel bound ethically to keep a confidence. But what if you want to publish information that might be confidential but you feel some greater public interest is served by disclosing it? The defence of 'just cause or excuse' or 'exposure of iniquity' addresses this situation. If the material has been disclosed by others under absolute privilege, as in court proceedings or in parliament, it can be the subject of a fair report and no breach of confidence occurs. Disclosure of confidential information can be defended on the grounds of 'justified disclosure' if there is a just cause or excuse. At the very least this means a confidence can be broken if it relates to a crime or fraud.

Beyond this, the courts have allowed the breach of a confidence in the public interest involving other kinds of misconduct that fall short of an actual crime or fraud. Attempts at applying this to the revelation of trivial secrets have failed, because their disclosure has been held not to be in the public interest. Some secrets might be revealed in the interests of community safety or health. The clear requirement is that there is some overriding public interest in the confidence being broken. In the eyes of the courts, mere public curiosity in the matter is not enough.

▶ **'So, what can they do to me?'**

If the unauthorised disclosure of a secret has already happened, a plaintiff will normally seek compensation or an 'account of profits'. An account of profits is a reimbursement to the plaintiff of profits the defendant has made through the use of the confidential information. But compensation is the more common remedy.

If the disclosure of the secret has not yet happened, the plaintiff will likely try to get an injunction preventing the disclosure. This might be a temporary or a permanent injunction. While the courts are reluctant to grant injunctions if an award of compensation will compensate the plaintiff satisfactorily, it is usually the gist of the plaintiff's complaint that publication will cause irreparable harm.

In a 2006 breach of confidence ruling about illicit drug use by Australian Rules football players, the Victorian Supreme Court issued a permanent injunction that still applies to Victorian citizens today.[10] The Australian Football League has a 'three strikes' policy: it will not reveal that players have used stimulants, narcotics or cannabis until the third time they have tested positive. Once word was out that some players had tested positive once or twice, journalists were set to name them. Their names had appeared on an Internet discussion forum, where one was said to have a 'nostril-related hamstring injury'. But despite the secret being broken there and in a digital version of a newspaper article, the court issued a permanent order that no such player could be identified—ever.

While courts in Commonwealth countries are often reluctant to restrain publication before a defamation suit, they are far more likely to issue an injunction where a breach of confidence is alleged. Bloggers could also face applications for orders to deliver up their files and reveal their sources.

▶ Shielding sources

Courts throughout the world have long insisted on witnesses answering relevant questions, whether or not they are bound by some professional or ethical obligation of silence. Lawyers are an exception. Throughout the UK, North America and the Commonwealth, a legal professional (attorney–client) privilege protects lawyers from having to reveal to the court prejudicial statements a client might have confided in them. In some places the privilege has been extended to doctor–patient relationships and sometimes to priests whose parishioners might have confessed criminal sins to them. Witnesses are also excused from answering incriminating questions in court. Sometimes, as in the Australian state of New South Wales under section 126B of the *Evidence Act*,[11] judges are given discretion to weigh up all professional confidences against the interests of justice in deciding whether a question must be answered.

Canada allows a promise of confidence to be protected in court if:

- It originates with a non-disclosure agreement.
- It is essential to the relationship involved.
- The relationship is one that should be fostered 'in the public good'.
- The public interest in protecting the identity of the informant outweighs the public interest at getting at the truth.

This was put to the test in Ontario in 2010, when the *National Post* newspaper was ordered to produce the documents upon which it had based corruption allegations against the prime minister.[12] Despite the newspaper's claim of a journalist–source confidential relationship, the Supreme Court decided there was no such constitutional right and that a greater public interest lay in pursuing an investigation that the source had actually forged the documents in question.

Several western democratic nations have also introduced so-called 'shield laws' that specifically excuse journalists from having to identify their confidential sources in court, and sometimes allow them to refuse to hand up their interview records or other documents. According to the Reporters Committee for Freedom of the Press, thirty-one US states and the District of Columbia have shield laws protecting journalists' confidential relationships with their sources, although several have quite serious limitations.[13] Britain offers limited protection for journalists in its 1981 *Contempt of Court Act*.[14] New Zealand's *Evidence Act* protects journalists' sources, but gives discretion to a judge to override this on public interest grounds.[15]

France amended its 1881 press law in early 2010 to protect the confidentiality of journalists' sources after pressure from Reporters Without Borders. This was enough for a Bordeaux appeal court to rule in 2011 that a prosecutor had wrongly allowed two *Le Monde* reporters' phone records to be seized when they were covering a high-profile case involving L'Oréal heiress Liliane Bettencourt.[16]

Yet a tough shield law in another European country was not enough to protect one reporter and blogger. Young Ukrainian journalist Olena Bilozerska had her cameras, computers, phone and other gear seized by police in Kiev despite Article 17 of the press law stating that 'journalists may not be arrested or detained in connection with their professional activities and their equipment may not be confiscated'. She was interrogated after posting footage of someone throwing a Molotov cocktail at a building during a protest.[17]

Journalists have been jailed in many countries for refusing to reveal their sources in court or hand over documents that might break confidences. Between 1984 and 2011, twenty-one US journalists were jailed under such laws, including video blogger Josh Wolf, who was released in 2007 after serving 226 days for refusing to hand over tape of protesters damaging a police car.[18] *New York Times* journalist Judith Miller served eighty-six days in prison in 2005 for refusing to tell a grand jury who leaked the identity of CIA operative Valerie Plame to the media.[19]

Three Australian journalists have been jailed and others charged for refusing to reveal their sources since the early 1990s.[20] The Committee to Protect Journalists records numerous other cases, including arrests in Ghana,[21] Ethiopia[22] and Kenya.[23]

▶ Bloggers and shield laws

The limited protections offered to journalists trying to keep their sources confidential, even in the US, are more restricted when it comes to bloggers and social media users. The shield laws vary widely in their scope, sometimes only applying to material that has already been 'published' and sometimes specifically naming 'journalists' and 'news media' as those protected. New federal shield laws introduced in Australia in 2011 extend to bloggers and tweeters—but only to those 'engaged and active in the publication of news'.[24]

Some US state shield laws can be interpreted to cover new media users, while others are narrowly construed to apply only to journalists in the mainstream media. Montana's shield laws were held to apply to anonymous Internet commenters in 2008 when a former political candidate launched a defamation action over material on the *Billings Gazette*'s site.[25] But another blogger who was sued for defamation over comments on a message board failed to win protection under the New Jersey shield law in 2011.[26] The application of Californian shield laws to bloggers was questioned in 2010 when Gizmodo gadget blog editor Jason Chen appeared in a video on the site displaying a prototype of an Apple iPhone 4, which had been lost then purchased by an intermediary for about US$5000. Police seized six computers and other items from Chen's home. But the matter was not tested when charges against Chen were not pursued.[27]

There were calls for a US federal shield law after travel bloggers Chris Elliott and Steve Frischling were subpoenaed in late 2009 during a search for the anonymous correspondent who had provided them with the Transportation Security Administration security directive they had posted after a failed terrorist attack. The TSA ultimately withdrew its subpoenas.[28]

▶ Whistleblower immunity

It is one thing for a journalist or blogger to get permission to keep a source confidential, but what about the sources themselves? Countries vary widely on whether whistleblowers can win protection from prosecution for revealing wrongdoing within their organisations or government departments. Sometimes this is the very reason someone sets up a blog—to blow the whistle on misbehaviour within a company or the bureaucracy.

In some places there are broad 'public interest' protections for whistleblowing about crime and corruption, just as there is the 'disclosure of iniquity' defence to breach of confidence we discussed earlier. In jurisdictions where anti-corruption agencies have been established, complete immunity is usually offered to witnesses coming forward to reveal wrongdoing. By the turn of this century, such laws were quite common in the US, Canada, the UK, South Africa, Australia and New Zealand.[29]

However, few countries offer protection to whistleblowers who bypass official channels and go directly to the media with their allegations or use online methods to leak confidential information in their efforts to expose criminal or unethical behaviour. Lancashire detective constable Richard Horton operated a blog under the pseudonym 'Night Jack', giving an insider's view on police work and his opinions on political issues. He went all the way to the High Court in an attempt to stop the *Times* from revealing his real identity. But Justice Eady ruled that the blog was a 'public activity' and that citizens also had a public interest in knowing that a police officer was making these sorts of communications.[30]

If approaches to the official channels are not available or have not worked, some jurisdictions allow whistle-blowers to go to the media with their allegations and retain immunity. That's the way it works under the *Public Interest Disclosures Act* in New South Wales, Australia.[31]

Some officials are just not savvy enough with social media and inadvertently leak confidential information when using Facebook or Twitter. That happened in the UK Ministry of Defence, which revealed it had disciplined several personnel for blabbing secrets on social media networks when they thought they were just chatting with 'friends'.[32]

▶ Common sense when dealing with whistleblowers

Despite such whistleblower protection laws, confidential sources face lengthy jail terms in most countries if they reveal state secrets, because officials might not agree there is an ethical or public interest in the material being revealed. That was certainly the case with one of the most famous whistleblowers of the modern era—the military analyst Daniel Ellsberg, who leaked the sensitive 'Pentagon Papers' regarding US involvement in Vietnam to the press in 1971.[33] Despite government efforts to stop the publication of the material, the Supreme Court allowed the *New York Times* and the *Washington Post* to go ahead with its release.[34] Ellsberg and a co-accused later faced charges of conspiracy, theft of government property and espionage, which were dismissed among allegations of FBI wiretapping.[35]

In the modern era it is even harder to protect communications against detection by the authorities, so you need to take extraordinary steps if you hope to keep your sources truly confidential. Geolocation technologies, phone records and security cameras are just some of the mechanisms agencies can use to determine who has been talking to the investigative journalist or blogger.

The international whistleblowing organisation WikiLeaks became famous for revealing the twenty-first-century equivalent of the Pentagon Papers when it released thousands of secret US government files on Middle East conflicts and broader diplomatic relations throughout 2010 and 2011. It reassured sources that its high-security encrypted submission system, using an electronic drop box, protected their identities. However, US soldier Bradley Manning was arrested in 2010 over the release of classified material to WikiLeaks and held in solitary confinement pending trial.

Yet the WikiLeaks saga might even have made the leaking of government secrets 'sexy', according to security experts quoted by the BBC.[36] It has created the perception that leaking confidential data was 'inherently good'. Hopefully, this chapter has shown you that trading in confidential information can be anything but sexy. Even experienced investigative journalists and organisations specifically set up for handling leaks can find the area a minefield.

Amateur bloggers and citizen journalists should pay heed to the fact that their colleagues have served jail time throughout the world for either leaking secrets or refusing to name their off-the-record sources in court. You might have all sorts of moral reasons for breaking a confidence in the public interest, but you should not do so frivolously and should first weigh up the potential repercussions very carefully.

IN BRIEF: CONFIDENTIALITY

- Celebrities will sometimes sue for breach of confidence if you have revealed something private about them.

- While confidentiality is closely entwined with privacy in Europe, there are strict laws of confidentiality in the US, the UK and its former colonies.

- If it seems to be confidential information, then it probably is. Talk to a lawyer before leaking it because you can face criminal charges or be sued.

- That said, there may be ways to defend a breach of confidence, particularly if it relates to a matter of genuine public interest.

- For breaches of commercial confidence, you might be called to account for any profits you have made out of blabbing someone's trade secrets.

- Journalists are protected by 'shield laws' in many places, meaning they might not have to reveal their confidential sources of information to the court. Only a few jurisdictions have opened this privilege up to bloggers.

- Public servants who 'blow the whistle' on corruption and wrongdoing are protected when they go through the appropriate channels, but they will usually not earn this immunity if they simply run to the media or go online with their secrets.

- Be extra careful if you are dealing in this area. Surveillance and monitoring is so prevalent and sophisticated today that it is very hard to keep any source confidential or secret.

CHAPTER 7

THE FINE LINE BETWEEN OPINION AND BIGOTRY

Twitbrief: Legal risks of online discrimination and hate speech #race #religion #blasphemy #Holocaust #gender #sexualpreference

When the Danish newspaper *Jyllands-Posten* printed twelve cartoons depicting Mohammed in 2005, its journalists knew there would be a reaction. The idea for the stunt had come about because a children's author had told them of the difficulty he was having finding someone to illustrate a book he was writing about the prophet's life.

But they could never have expected the religious, economic and criminal backlash that would be unleashed. Within months the images had spread via the Internet and scores of other newspapers, triggering protests in which more than 100 people died, and prompting flag-burning, the bombing and arson of Danish embassies, the declaration of a fatwa by Muslim clerics and an axe attack on one of the cartoonists.

The cartoons had seemed like a good idea at the time to the newspaper's culture editor, Flemming Rose, who wanted to 'integrate Muslims into the Danish tradition of satire', he wrote in the *Washington Post*.[1] Instead, this became one of the most divisive actions by a media outlet in modern history.

The free expression traditions of Denmark clashed directly with an ancient Sunni Muslim prohibition on the visual illustration of Mohammed. The depiction of the prophet with an ignited fuse in his headdress sparked the most heated reaction from devotees.

Several years have passed since the cartoons were first published, but the original cartoonists and editors—as well as those who reproduced them in other newspapers and online—still hold well-founded fears of retribution for their actions.

The Danish cartoons episode was not the first time Muslims had taken offence at material they deemed blasphemous. The most famous fatwa was against British author Salman Rushdie in 1989, when Iranian leader Ayatollah Ruhollah Khomeini sentenced him to death for writing the novel *The Satanic Verses*. The book was based loosely on the life of Mohammed. The Japanese translator was stabbed to death in 1991 and the Italian translator was also stabbed. In 1993 the Norwegian publisher of the book was shot outside his Oslo home.

In another media-sparked riot, more than 200 died in protests in 2002 when a Nigerian newspaper suggested the prophet could have taken his pick of Miss World contestants during a debate over whether the nation should have been hosting the pageant.[2]

Hopefully, by the end of this chapter you will only put any truly inflammatory views out there after carefully weighing the potential implications.

▶ **A cultural and political war zone in your pocket**
The Danish journalists acted well within the laws of their own country when they decided to publish the cartoons, but by the time the words and images had spread on the Internet, they found themselves in direct conflict with official and sharia laws in some Muslim states. They became objects of hatred and targets for revenge.

Sadly, human beings have found the negative energy to hate each other since time immemorial. Hatred of one form or another explains most of the wars and acts of violence throughout history. While the Internet and social media have allowed us to communicate with countless new friends and form all kinds of new relationships, we do not just attract the attention of the 'like-minded'.

There is a war going on in our pockets and handbags, on each and every smartphone, and on every home computer connected to the Net. There are people so possessed with loathing that they are conducting a cyberwar on the objects of their disdain.

No matter who you are and where you live, there are others who might not know you personally but will hate you for the category of human being you are: black, white, Asian, Hispanic, male, female, transgender, gay, straight, conservative, liberal, environmentalist, climate change denier, Muslim, Jew, Christian, atheist, obese, American, British, Pakistani, teenager, elderly, rich, poor, lawyer, politician or used car salesman. (Lucky there's not a 'hate' button on Facebook.)

Sometimes even some fun turns sour. A satirical swipe at redheads on the *South Park* television series prompted a fourteen-year-old Canadian boy to set up a Facebook 'Kick a Ginger' campaign in 2008, rapidly joined by more than 5000 fans. As the *Telegraph* reported, dozens of children posted comments on the page claiming to have attacked redheads, with a thirteen-year-old girl from Alberta and her sister among the victims of the schoolyard bullies.[3]

Some people judge you based on the labels they apply to you rather than who you really are or the life experiences that inform your views and values—and they are online and angry.

If you also have strong opinions and express them without fear or favour, your challenge is to avoid becoming one of them. If you do, the force of the law in most places can be brought down upon you.

▶ Personal vendettas

Some individuals just cannot back away from a fight, in real life or cyberspace. They become so obsessed with their causes or grudges that they launch poisonous online assaults on others that can leave their targets as traumatised as they would have been if they had been assaulted physically. Tragically, some victims have become so despairing and fearful that they have been driven to take their own lives.

In the eyes of the law, such attacks go under a range of names according to their type, scale and jurisdiction. They include: cyberbullying, cyberstalking, online trolling, malicious online content, using carriage services to menace, harassment, hate speech, vilification, discrimination and even assault. Some are criminal offences for which offenders can be fined or jailed; others are civil wrongs for which courts can award damages to victims. Some are litigated under actions we have already considered, such as defamation, breach of privacy and breach of confidentiality.

Some of these attacks are difficult to explain because the motivations are beyond the imagination of ordinary citizens. Australian Bradley Hampson served 220 days in jail in 2011 for plastering obscene images and comments on Facebook tribute pages dedicated to the memory of two children who had died in tragic circumstances. He had entered the sites to depict a penis near one victim's mouth and made offensive comments including 'Woot I'm Dead' and 'Had It Coming'. Hampson had been convicted of a similar offence three years earlier.[4]

At about the same time, the US Appeals court in Virginia was dealing with a suit by former high school senior Kara Kowalski, who had been suspended for five days for creating a MySpace page called 'S.A.S.H'.[5] She claimed it stood for 'Students Against Sluts Herpes', but the court found it really aimed to ridicule a fellow student named Shay. Kowalski had also incurred a social suspension for ninety days, preventing her from cheerleading and from crowning her successor in the school's 'Charm Review'. She felt aggrieved at the suspension, claiming it had violated her constitutional free speech and due process rights as the page had not been created during school time and was really 'private, out of school speech'. But the court disagreed.

'Kowalski's role in the "S.A.S.H." webpage, which was used to ridicule and demean a fellow student, was particularly mean-spirited and hateful,' Judge Niemeyer wrote. 'The webpage called on classmates, in a pack, to target Shay N., knowing that it would be hurtful and damaging to her ability to sit with other students in class at Musselman High School and have a suitable learning experience.' The court agreed with the school and the trial judge that 'such harassment and bullying is inappropriate and hurtful' and denied her damages claim. The 'Queen of Charm' indeed!

▶ **Rights infringements**

International conventions, national constitutions and bills of rights underpin the laws protecting citizens throughout the world from hatred and discrimination. These laws equip bloggers and social media users with defences against spiteful attacks, but they simultaneously offer protection to those insulted by offensive blog posts or tweets. At the highest level, Article 2 of the Universal Declaration of Human Rights counsels against the withdrawal of rights based on citizens' views or backgrounds:

> Everyone is entitled to all the rights and freedoms set forth in this Declaration, without distinction of any kind, such as race, colour, sex, language, religion, political or other opinion, national or social origin, property, birth or other status.

Article 7 warns against discrimination:

> All are equal before the law and are entitled without any discrimination to equal protection of the law. All are entitled to equal protection against any discrimination in violation of this Declaration and against any incitement to such discrimination.

Article 18 confers the right to 'freedom of thought, conscience and religion'. As we have found with other areas of social media law, all of these rights need to be balanced against Article 19's 'right to freedom of opinion and expression . . . [including] freedom to hold opinions without interference'.

Similar expressions can be found in the European Convention on Human Rights, the American Declaration of the Rights and Duties of Man, the American Convention on Human Rights, and numerous national constitutions.

And that's the challenge facing courts and legislators developing anti-discrimination, cyberbullying and hate speech laws throughout the world: countries have found different points of balance for these rights. In the US, for example, there is a strong First Amendment protection even for hateful speech, and the Supreme Court has struck down lower court decisions and state legislation attempting to gag free expression. By contrast, Germany and several other European countries have Holocaust denial laws, under which revisionist historians and neo-Nazis have been jailed for expressing their views.[6]

▶ Hate speech and hate sites

Hatred features in the International Covenant on Civil and Political Rights at Article 20, which prohibits 'Any advocacy of national, racial or religious hatred that constitutes incitement to discrimination, hostility or violence'. Despite these words, the Simon Wiesenthal Center in New York logged at least 14,000 'hate sites' on the Internet in 2011.[7] A browse through Raymond A. Franklin's Hate Directory of some of the main ones makes for disturbing reading.[8]

Social media has helped far-right extremists connect with each other and fuel intolerance and outright hatred against any ethnic, religious or political group in their sights.

'Fifty years ago, if you believed that the Earth was populated by spies from Jupiter, it would have taken you quite some time to find someone else who shared the same belief,' Bob Ayers, a London-based former US intelligence official, told the *Globe and Mail*. 'That's not the case today. Social networking sites have changed the mathematics of things, and with that change, comes both pros and cons.'

You're allowed to hate in the US.

One such hate site was the subject of a US District Court decision in 2011. Judge Lynn Adelman had to consider the free expression rights of a neo-Nazi who was charged with using a website to call for violence against a juror. William White had set up the site Overthrow. com, affiliated with the American National Socialist Workers Party. The group's membership consisted of white supremacists. On the site, White ranted against 'non-whites, Jews, homosexuals, and persons perceived by white supremacists as acting contrary to the interests of the white race'. He advocated violence against the 'enemies' of white supremacy.[9]

White became especially riled about the 480-month sentence handed out to fellow neo-Nazi Matthew Hale for obstructing justice and solicitation. He wrote that everyone associated with the Hale trial 'has deserved assassination for a long time'. He then targeted one of the jurors, whom he identified on his website by name and photo. White wrote:

> Gay Jewish anti-racist Mark P Hoffmann was a
> juror who played a key role in convicting Hale.
> Born August 24, 1964, he lives at [full address]
> with his gay black lover and his cat 'homeboy'.

He listed Hoffmann's home, office and cell phone numbers. It all sat under the heading 'Gay Jewish Anti-Racist Led Jury'. White was then charged and convicted of 'soliciting or otherwise endeavouring to persuade another person to injure Hoffman based on his jury service in the Hale case'.

But Judge Adelman allowed his appeal on the grounds that he had not made a direct call to violence against the juror and that as a result White's speech had First Amendment protection. Judge Adelman explained that the US Constitution 'protects vehement, scathing, and offensive criticism of others, including individuals involved in the criminal justice system, such as Juror Hoffman'. He ruled that even speech advocating law-breaking was protected unless it was directed at inciting immediate lawless action and was likely to prompt it. Even Internet communications disclosing personal information about other citizens that might alarm or intimidate them or 'expose them to unwanted attention from others' was protected in the US.

'We live in a democratic society founded on fundamental constitutional principles,' Judge Adelman said. 'In this society, we do not quash fear by increasing government power, proscribing those constitutional principles, and silencing those speakers of whom the majority disapproves.'

The decision sits with earlier Supreme Court hate speech judgments, which have found that all but communications integral to criminal conduct—fighting words, threats and solicitations—have free expression protection in America. The US government can't stop people burning crosses to express their views, but it can legislate to stop them burning those same crosses to intimidate other citizens. This means extremists like Nazis and Ku Klux Klan members are allowed to advocate the use of force, but can't incite imminent criminal actions.

▶ **Confusion north of the border**

Canadian human rights lawyer Richard Warman has been conducting his own legal campaign against hate speech by extremists. (Results of a Google search of his name show the level of hateful reaction he has received!) He has won fifteen cases at the Canadian Human Rights Tribunal since 2001, with injunctions issued to restrain hate speech and penalties and damages totalling C$95,000 ordered from extremists.[10] He was behind Canada's first finding of liability against an ISP because it had failed to remove hateful material despite knowing it was there.[11] His actions also prompted the Federal Court to issue its first injunction over Internet hate, followed by a jail sentence for contempt for an extremist who refused to comply. Warman also won a case to reveal the identities of two anonymous John Does who had defamed him, as we saw in Chapter 4.

But a 2009 decision by the Tribunal was a setback for Warman because it ruled that hate speech was protected by the free expression provision of the Charter of Rights and Freedoms. Warman's complaint was against Marc

Lemire, webmaster of freedomsite.org. He claimed messages on the site were discriminatory and violated the Canadian *Human Rights Act* by exposing minority groups to 'hatred and contempt'. Section 13 of the *Human Rights Act* says it is 'discriminatory' to communicate 'any matter that is likely to expose a person or persons to hatred or contempt' over their race, religion, sexual orientation, or a range of other characteristics.[12] The site included a poem describing non-white immigrants as 'trash' because they purportedly abused the welfare system, drove down property values and made a 'hobby' of breeding. But Lemire argued that the material was satirical and that the law was inconsistent with the Charter's freedom of expression provisions. Tribunal member Athanasios Hadjis agreed, so the issue headed for appeal.[13]

All section 13 cases have since been suspended by the Canadian Human Rights Commission, pending the outcome of a legal review.

▶ Hate speech elsewhere

Free expression does not trump hateful cyberspeech in most other countries. In fact, in some parts of the world, history has helped shape particularly tough hate speech restrictions. Special laws against the denial of the Holocaust have resulted in jail terms for some individuals. Australian revisionist historian Dr Frederick Töben, founder and director of the Adelaide Institute, was jailed in Germany for publishing material on the Internet casting doubt that the Holocaust—the murder of hundreds of thousands of Jewish people in gas chambers during the Second World War—actually happened, and claiming that some Jewish people had exaggerated facts about it for financial gain.[14] Following his jail sentence, he published further Holocaust denial material to the Institute's website. The president of the Executive Council of Australian Jewry, Jeremy Jones, then won a finding in the Human Rights and Equal Opportunity Commission that the publication breached the *Racial Discrimination Act*. He applied to the Federal Court of Australia, asking that the commission's determination be enforced. Töben was subsequently found guilty of contempt and sentenced to three months' imprisonment.

Yahoo! found itself in court on both sides of the Atlantic in 2000 and 2006 over its posting of ads for hundreds of Nazi symbols and objects. The webpages featured links to Adolf Hitler's autobiography, *Mein Kampf*, along with other anti-Semitic material, Nazi web-auction sites and sites maintained by Holocaust denial groups. A French court ruled that Yahoo! had violated France's hate speech laws by displaying the material. The judge also ordered the Californian company to take down links from its primary site, yahoo.com. Its daily fine against Yahoo! for failing to comply totalled about US$15 million by 2006. The company voluntarily took down some of the material, but went to court in the US arguing the judgment could not be enforced there. A US appeals court rejected Yahoo!'s bid to have the French order ruled unenforceable on jurisdictional grounds, and the Supreme Court refused to consider a further appeal. [15]

Facebook also appeared torn over the issue of Holocaust denial sites. It removed some sites in 2009 but ignored others, claiming they did not breach its terms of service.[16]

Of course, not all religious hate cases involve anti-Semitism. A Scottish football fan turned especially nasty in 2011, setting up websites where sectarian hate messages were posted about the manager of the Celtics team.[17] Ian Rooney, twenty-four, was charged with breach of the peace with religious aggravation. The BBC quoted the head of the Football Co-ordination Unit, Superintendent David Brand, as saying:

> I would advise anyone who has posted messages which are likely or intended to threaten violence or cause fear or alarm to any person to remove them immediately. We are not only targeting those who post messages on the Internet but those who seek to create Internet hate sites. Please be warned, if you do post hatred over the Internet, you may not be arrested today, but we will be paying you a visit some time in the future.[18]

Anti-Islamic comments on websites, Internet forums, in newspapers and in a short film resulted in far-right Dutch politician Geert Wilders facing five counts of hate speech and discrimination in 2011. The *Telegraph* reported that Wilders argued he was 'obliged to speak' because of the Islamic 'threat' in the Netherlands. Wilders was acquitted on all counts, with Judge Marcel van Oosten ruling his statements were 'acceptable within the context of the public debate'. 'The bench finds that although gross and degenerating, it did not give rise to hatred,' the judge declared.[19]

▶ OMG...

The law of blasphemy exists in various forms throughout the world, covering a range of offences that are seen as insulting to a religion. In some countries it is a criminal offence to doubt or deny the existence of God or Allah, or to criticise prophets or religious laws such as sharia.

The UN High Commissioner for Human Rights, Navi Pillay, summed up the dilemma with such laws following the assassination of two leading Pakistani politicians on religious grounds. 'Experience around the world has shown that blasphemy laws often become a double edged sword,' she said. 'While aimed at protecting certain values they are open to abuse and lead to violations of freedom of expression, freedom of religion and ultimately the right to life.'[20]

Muslim countries such as Iran, Afghanistan and Pakistan draw on sharia law for tough punishments for any behaviour deemed blasphemous. The International Humanist and Ethical Union also drew attention to criminal laws in the African states of Nigeria, Algeria, Egypt, Tunisia and Sudan, where offenders can be jailed or even executed for blasphemous statements or actions.

While Islamic states have their own versions—as the Danish cartoonists learned—the ancient English version involving an insult to the Christian faith still exists in some former British colonies. In New Zealand, for example, you can be jailed for up to a year for 'blasphemous libel', although the crime was last prosecuted in 1922.[21] The UK abolished its blasphemy laws in 2008. There has not been a successful prosecution for blasphemy in England since 1977, when moral campaigner Mary Whitehouse brought a private prosecution against the publisher of

Gay News for printing a poem about a Roman centurion's love for Jesus.

Several European countries also retain blasphemy laws, although they are rarely prosecuted. A German political activist was issued a suspended sentence in 2006 for distributing toilet paper on which he had written words from the Koran.[22]

Whether you are a satirist or a political or religious activist, you should consider the potential consequences carefully before blogging or tweeting anything that might be considered a religious insult.

▶ Race hate—not just a black and white issue

While some hate sites and social media users focus on religious attacks, others specialise in vilifying others because of their racial or ethnic backgrounds.

A Canadian prisoner used his Facebook page to upload a video taunting inmates who had assaulted him with weightlifting equipment during a jailhouse riot in 2011.[23] Canada.com reported that convicted armed robber Joshua Erdodi used racist slurs as he reclined in his hospital bed and spoke to camera in the thirty-second clip. 'Fuck you, n—ers,' he said, flipping his middle finger at the camera before half-heartedly retracting the statement. 'Just kidding, just kidding,' he said, snickering. 'I don't want no more stabbings.' The Correctional Service of Canada was investigating whether he had committed a hate crime by making the comments.

Even worse comments were deemed protected in a US Court of Appeal decision in mid-2011. Californian Walter Bagdasarian had been convicted of online threats against then presidential candidate Barack Obama two weeks before his election in November 2008. Bagdasarian had placed comments on the Yahoo! Finance site, calling Obama a 'n—er' and saying, 'he will have a 50 cal in the head soon.' He then went even further: 'Shoot the n—er.' A member of the forum tipped off Secret Service agents and Bagdasarian was sentenced to two months' jail over two counts of criminal threats to a presidential candidate. But the appeals court majority held that while the statements were 'repugnant', they had not been proven to represent a 'true threat' to Obama, and thereby qualified for First Amendment protection.[24] Judge Kim McClane Wardlaw dissented, writing: 'History undermines the conclusion that a reasonable person would interpret Mr. Bagdasarian's "50 cal in the head" comment as a joke or mere political rhetoric.' She pointed to the recent shooting of Arizona representative Gabrielle Giffords as an example of where a bizarre Internet comment could foreshadow true danger.

Laws in Australia's nine jurisdictions deal with hate speech in different ways and with varying levels of intensity, with Western Australia focusing on the publication of material intended to incite racial hatred or to harass people of a racial group. Some state laws prohibit any public act inciting hatred or even severe ridicule of an individual or a group because of race. Defences of public interest, fair comment and privilege vary across jurisdictions, but usually apply in a similar way to defamation defences.[25]

▶ Straight lies for queer guys and gals

Sexual preference is another source of hate speech on the Internet, with blogs and social media used to harass, 'out' and generally make life difficult for homosexuals, sometimes even prompting suicides. In 2011, nineteen-year-old Rutgers University student Dharun Ravi faced fifteen criminal counts of bias intimidation and invasion of privacy after his Internet activities were blamed for the suicide of Tyler Clementi. The eighteen-year-old freshman had jumped from the George Washington Bridge after Ravi had posted a live video stream of his intimate encounter with another man and advertised it on Twitter.[26] The incident prompted a number of high-profile figures, including President Barack Obama and talk show host Ellen DeGeneres, to denounce cyberbullying. This was one of the more extreme examples of people using social media to 'out' homosexuals.

Gossip blogger Perez Hilton also came under attack for outing boy band star Lance Bass in 2006. The former *NSYNC star was forced to go public in *People* magazine to formally announce his sexuality after he became one of several celebrities Hilton decided to target.[27]

In the UK, *X-Factor* winner Joe McElderry expressed relief to be able to be honest about his sexuality after a prankster hacked into his Twitter account and outed him. 'I think the Twitter thing was the point when I realised I was gay,' he told the *Sun*. 'It is a liberating feeling. Now I can get on with the rest of my life and move on and be comfortable.'[28]

Despite this happy outcome, bloggers and social media users should not rush to tell the world about the sexual preferences of others. Privacy, harassment and anti-discrimination laws in many countries can make it a very expensive form of gossip.

In Australia, for example, two talkback radio hosts were found to be in breach of the anti-vilification provisions of the New South Wales *Anti-Discrimination Act* when they described homosexuals as 'poofs' engaged in 'grubby activities'.[29] But a later incident, when radio announcer John Laws described the host of *Queer Eye for the Straight Guy* as a 'pompous little pansy', a 'pillow-biting pompous little prig' and a 'precious little pansy', the comments were ruled to have been made in good faith under a public interest defence.[30]

Facebook was accused of privacy breaches in 2010, when it was revealed that users received different kinds of advertising according to whether they had nominated themselves as 'straight' or 'gay' on the social network's profile settings.[31]

▶ Moderating your online comments

There are, of course, other types of hate speech and other target groups. As a social media user, you will sometimes have strong views that you feel you must express. One of the beauties of Web 2.0 is that you can do so quickly and effortlessly. The lesson of this chapter is that you should pause and think before you post. Consider the potential impacts on those you are targeting . . . and ponder the possible consequences for your own bank balance, freedom and safety if you post a particularly offensive comment in a jurisdiction without First Amendment protections. In the US, you need to draw the line at any incitement to crime or violence, but that's just to defend a court case—your personal safety is another issue.

IN BRIEF: FREE SPEECH

- One person's free expression is another's discrimination or vilification. Bear this in mind when you blog or tweet on the prickly issues of race, religion, gender, sexual preference and other topics that could offend.

- Beware of jokes and satire. Others often don't get the joke and might interpret your satirical writing as your heartfelt opinion.

- If you are so fired up about a topic that you are shooting off flames of vitriol targeted at individuals or groups, think seriously about getting some counselling before you are sued or charged with a criminal offence. (While Web 2.0 is a wonderful vehicle to push a barrow or pursue a cause, it is dangerous to embark on vendettas.)

- Anti-discrimination is protected at the highest level, with the Universal Declaration of Human Rights enshrining freedom of thought, conscience and religion. Weigh this up against any right to free expression you may have.

- Most countries have strong laws against hate speech. The US is an exception, with hate speech protected unless it is intimidating other citizens directly or openly calling upon others to commit a crime.

- European countries are particularly sensitive to online writing denying the Holocaust. Jail terms apply.

- Blasphemy laws in many countries carry heavy penalties for insults to God and religious beliefs. Take special care with any criticism of the Koran or any visual depiction of Allah.

- Before posting that inflammatory, racist, bigoted message (even if it is within the bounds of your country's laws), just remember that not everyone chooses to resolve their disputes in the courts. Your personal safety may well be in danger.

CHAPTER 8

COPYCATS AND CORPORATE CAPERS

Twitbrief: IP and corporate dangers for online writers #copyright #IP #moralrights #trademarks #publicityrights #freeuse #workplaceblogs #domains

Los Angeles-based brand manager and copywriter Rachel Kane, twenty-six, was a regular shopper at Forever 21—a major fashion retailer specialising in the latest look at the cheapest prices. She found some of their outfits so ungainly and wacky that she set up a hilarious single-topic blog called WTForever 21 to post photos of some of the most bizarre examples with her own satirical comments. But the fashion conglomerate didn't share her sense of humour and its lawyers sent her two cease-and-desist letters, demanding she take down the site.

> Your website's name refers to an abbreviation for colloquial expression that the general public may find offensive, and such colloquial expression is being used in conjunction with our Company's

name, registered trademark, and domain name . . .
Please note we consider such conduct and other
use in your website to infringe upon and dilute the
Company's trademarks. Also, you utilise images
from our Company's website without permission,
which infringes on the Company's copyrights in
those images.[1]

Kane's first instinct was to give in to the demands and
remove her site, but after taking legal advice and rallying
support from the online media, she called their bluff,
blogging:

Dear Lovers of Gnarly Fashion:

After two legally baseless cease-and-desist letters
from Forever 21, two painstakingly researched
responses, and zero substantive replies from
Forever 21's legal team, I have no choice but to
interpret the company's non-responsiveness as an
admission that my blog, WTForever21.com, does
not infringe any of Forever 21's rights.

Through my attorneys [. . .] I recently imposed
my own deadline on Forever 21 which the company
has failed to meet. My attorneys and I will not
permit Forever 21 to use silence as a strategic
tool or intimidation tactic, particularly when the
company stood idly by *for over a year* as I blogged
about their design disasters.

As such, please enjoy today's long-overdue
offering of WTFashions. This is a dark defeat for
MC Hammer pants, floral jumpsuits and blinged
out mini hats, but a joyous triumph for those who

like to make fun of them. Which is pretty much anyone with eyes.

With love and lulz,
Rachel[2]

Both parties' deadlines passed without court action, but only time will tell whether Kane's defiant stance has paid off. The publicity hasn't done her blog any harm—it has since been featured in the Style section of the *Huffington Post*.[3] Either way, the case highlights the legal challenges independent bloggers can face when they ruffle the feathers of corporate giants.

▶ We're swimming in the same virtual ocean as the corporate sharks

While most bloggers and social media users do their online writing just for fun, you might be a single posting away from the corporate world of commercial litigation and highly valued intellectual property rights. You can also enter a legal quagmire if you are blogging, tweeting or posting Facebook messages as part of your work or just engaging in social media during your work time. If you are a professional blogger, solicit business online or host a website for an organisation, you should seek legal advice on your exposure to a host of commercial law issues in your jurisdiction: your personal liability when posting for your company; your contractual obligations; and the impact of trade practices, advertising and consumer laws on your work. Here are some basic intellectual property (IP) principles and a few of the traps other bloggers have encountered in the workplace.

▶ Bloggers and intellectual property (IP)

As an online writer—whether a blogger, tweeter, Facebook user or cyberjournalist—you can find yourself on either side of the intellectual property fence. If you place a high value on the merit of your words or images, you are probably not impressed when you discover someone else has cut and pasted them and pretended they are their own creations. On the other hand, you will often want to draw upon someone else's work and might even want to reproduce it in full. Sometimes you might want to stake your own claim to intellectual property rights and on other occasions you might need to defend your use of someone else's material.

Intellectual property laws are meant to protect our right to the exclusive use of the array of creative outputs we might produce as human beings. As a blogger, the IP area you have likely heard about is copyright, which covers creative works such as writing, music and images and in many countries also includes works of technology such as computer programs and databases. As a creator, you are granted property rights over the form of your expression. Most laws and treaties do not mention multimedia products, but experts agree their unique arrangement of sound, text and images also qualifies them for copyright protection as creative works.

Other types of intellectual property you might encounter online include performances and broadcasts, inventions and discoveries, industrial designs, trademarks and commercial names—all listed in 1967's Convention Establishing the World Intellectual Property Organisation. Put simply, IP comprises 'creations of the mind': inventions, literary and artistic works, and symbols, names, images and designs used in commerce.

IP is a strange legal beast. It has a strong international foundation in treaties and conventions, with some common elements that apply no matter where you are based or where your material is accessed. Most of the world's nations are members of the Geneva-based World Intellectual Property Organisation (WIPO) and are signatories to the major treaties. International co-operation on IP laws dates back to the creation of the first international conventions covering industrial property, in Paris in 1883, and literary and artistic works, in Berne in 1886.

But elements of the law and its level of enforcement vary markedly between nations. IP can be one of the most complex areas of law, with specialists earning their living from advising clients on the intricacies of IP in particular jurisdictions, particularly as new technologies spawn an array of creations and the Internet highlights the technical differences forcing bewildering interpretations from the courts. It all means you really do need to seek expert legal advice if you are considering pushing the boundaries of IP law in your writing, or if you have already been threatened with legal action. You can find information about IP laws in your own country by browsing the Directory of Intellectual Property Offices.[4] The US Copyright Office, for example, has a useful introduction to that area of IP law and details US requirements at www.copyright.gov.

▶ Copyright—common global principles

Almost everything you might include in a blog is likely to be covered by copyright law—either you or another creator will hold the IP rights. That could include the words you post, illustrations or cartoons you draw, photographs or moving footage you upload, plans you draft, annotated lists you compile and music you share. Since time immemorial, some people have been tempted to steal the creative work of others, but it has been the introduction of copy-and-paste capabilities in computer software over the past three decades that has made copyright theft so easy and widespread.

The starting point for understanding copyright is that it does not protect an *idea* alone. (You need to look to industrial property laws for protection of inventions or ideas via patent law.) Copyright will only protect the *form of expression* used to convey your idea. So you might tweet about a brilliant concept you have for a new television drama series and then feel betrayed when someone beats you to the network to pitch that same proposal. The courts will just say 'bad luck', unless you can show that your rival has copied the words you used in your original treatment. The lesson here is that you shouldn't use blogs or social media to float ideas you want to protect.

The WIPO booklet 'Understanding Copyright and Related Rights' is an excellent entry-point for learning about the basic copyright principles that apply globally. The booklet explains that 'copyright' translates into 'author's rights' in many other languages because it is the creator of the work—the 'author' of written works—who holds the right to reproduce their outputs. The word 'copyright' in English refers to that act itself—the 'right' to 'copy' something you have created. As the holder of that right, you have the legal power to license others to do so as well.[5]

Most countries confer upon you a right to the exclusive use of your literary or artistic work the instant you create it—without the need for any kind of registration of the work as your own. You can use it in any way you like—as long as you do not break other laws in the process—and you also have the exclusive right to authorise others to use it and to charge them for that use. You can prohibit or authorise the reproduction of your work in a range of formats, the distribution of copies of your work, its public performance, its broadcast or communication to the public in other ways, its translation into another language and its adaptation from one format to another.

▶ **Copyright—important international differences**
First up, let's dispel a myth. A work does *not* have to display the copyright symbol '©' to be protected by copyright. Of course, it doesn't hurt to include it alongside your name and the year of creation, because there are still a few countries that are not signatories to the Berne Convention, which did away with the need to display it. Inserting '©' at least signals your claim of authorship to anyone who might think that because you posted material on the Internet or in social media, you are giving up your rights to its use.

An important difference between countries' copyright laws is duration. Under international conventions, your blog will remain copyright until at least fifty years after your death, although that is exactly half a century more than will concern you. But some countries, including the US and Australia—as well as all nations in the European Union—have extended this term to seventy years after the death of the creator. Of course, this rule is more relevant if you want to reproduce the work of a famous writer, artist or musician on your own blog. You will need to check whether enough time has passed after the author has died for the work to have entered the public domain, or whether the creator has voluntarily waived his or her rights by assigning a general licence to a copyright-free organisation.

The not-for-profit Creative Commons organisation is a good example of this.[6] Founded in 2001, it promotes the 'creative re-use of intellectual and artistic works', whether owned or in the public domain. It offers free copyright licences that enable creators to grant a voluntary 'some rights reserved' approach as an alternative to the traditional 'all rights reserved' default system of copyright law. Its public domain tools allow works that are free of known copyright to be easily searched online and provide a mechanism for rights-holders to dedicate their works to the public domain.

Some countries, such as the US, offer you several advantages if you have paid to register your copyright work with a federal government agency. For example, you can't file suit for infringement of your copyright in the US unless you have paid the registration fee. Australia does not have such a registration system.

▶ **Free use, fair use and fair dealing**
The law in most places allows for certain situations in which you can copy parts of other creators' material without their authorisation but with appropriate attribution. WIPO gives three key examples of such 'free use', which cover the purposes of many bloggers:

- quoting from a protected work, provided that the source of the quotation and the name of the author is mentioned, and that the extent of the quotation is compatible with fair practice;
- use of works by way of illustration for teaching purposes; and
- use of works for the purpose of news reporting.[7]

Some countries extend this to 'fair use' or 'fair dealing' defences. Of course, the courts and legislators in different countries vary in the way they interpret your 'fair' practice in borrowing such material, especially in relation to the proportion of the material you are copying. They also take into account how you have used the material, your purpose in doing so, the type of work you are copying, whether you are doing it for commercial gain, and the impact of your use upon the future commercial worth of the material. Fair dealing defences can apply to uses such as the reporting of news and current affairs, criticism and review, parody and satire, and education—depending on the jurisdiction and its laws.

Two of the most common copyright breaches on blogs are the posting of photos and the streaming of audio created by others. While the practice is common, and in some circumstances there will be a fair use defence available, your safest course is always to get the permission of the creator to reuse their material or to pay them for it. Often that means some detective work on your part because images in particular are copied so quickly on the Internet that it can be difficult to find out who the original creator or copyright-holder is. If it proves too difficult, you are wiser to create your own material. If that proves a tall order, it reinforces the creative worth of the work you were going to copy.

Full attribution of the creator is always essential to a fair use argument. The BBC was criticised in the *British Journal of Photography* for crediting Twitpic rather than the actual creators of the photographs it had broadcast during the London riots in 2011.[8] An example of an audio breach involved celebrity blogger Perez Hilton, who settled out of court with Zomba Recording, owner of the copyright to pop singer Britney Spears' music, after he had allegedly uploaded unreleased Spears tracks to his site.[9]

▶ Can you breach copyright in just 140 characters?

There has been debate over whether short Facebook and 140-character Twitter posts are subject to copyright at all. There are arguments that they would need to be particularly creative and unique—in the same way as a Japanese haiku poem—to win copyright protection in some places.[10] Certainly, mundane or trivial postings such as 'Just having coffee with friends at Central Latte' or 'President visiting here tomorrow' would be unlikely to qualify, partly because copyright does not cover simple factual material, only its form of expression. Also, the very nature of Twitter as a sharing medium—where you expect and even hope your banter will be retweeted—raises questions over the extent of attribution necessary and even possible.

▶ Transferring your copyright to others

If you are a blogger or a cyberjournalist working for a media corporation or selling your work on a freelance basis, you might not qualify for ongoing copyright royalties from your employers or clients. This is because some countries have passed laws to assign the employer automatic copyright in work they have paid you to produce. Sometimes this is limited under legislation to certain uses of the material—for example, for digital reproduction rather than photocopying—but you should always check to see whether you have any entitlement. If you sell your work on a freelance basis, you should find the answer in the contracts you have signed with whoever has commissioned your work. Such contracts often demand you sign over copyright as part of the deal and detail any limitations. You should look over this carefully with your lawyer because it could be that you are owed substantial back-payments of royalties if you have not signed away your entitlements.

Jurisdictions also vary on whether they allow you to assign selectively the rights to reproduce your work in certain ways and not others. For example, you might negotiate with a major media group to use your blog as a one-off column in the print version of their newspaper, but not assign them the right to reproduce it on their website. Of course, if you assign all rights to that media outlet, it then becomes the new owner of the copyright in that work.

Elsewhere, you are only allowed to 'license' others to use your work for a certain time and purpose, but you continue to own the copyright. As WIPO explains, 'the author of a novel may grant a license to a publisher to make and distribute copies of his work. At the same time, he may grant a license to a film producer to make a film based on the novel'.[11]

▶ Catch me if you can

Digital theft of creative work is rampant on the Internet and social media, as most of us know from the music, gaming and software piracy programs that have emerged over recent years. Some thieves have been pursued in court in either criminal prosecutions or civil actions. Both options are valid. Authorities will normally only prosecute under the criminal law and fine or jail the perpetrators if the theft has happened on a large commercial scale. But private individuals and companies have the option to sue for damages for breach of copyright in their courts if they can identify and serve a defendant.

And that's often the problem—finding the John or Jane Doe who has reproduced the material without your permission and then, even if you do win a judgment against them, actually extracting compensation.

The enforcement of intellectual property laws varies markedly throughout the world, as you have probably witnessed in the form of pirated designer-label clothing and bootleg DVDs openly on sale in the streets of some developing countries. For some creators, there is little that can be done to preserve the creative value of their work once it has been reproduced brazenly online. As a blogger, you have a moral obligation to your fellow creators to work within the allowable fair dealing provisions and make full acknowledgment of their original authorship.

▶ Is linking in breach?

Courts throughout the world have turned their attention to whether you are breaching copyright by linking to copyright material or linking to sites that infringe on someone's copyright. There has been a wide range of outcomes, so you should follow the decisions in your own jurisdiction closely and take legal advice if you are in any doubt about the risks involved by linking to other material.

However, taking into account all the linking that happens on an hourly basis via social media sites such as Facebook and Twitter, there seems to be very little risk in the practice for any single blogger. Most of the cases have centred on large-scale deep-linking to commercially valuable material within competitors' websites, particularly when it involves the 'mining' of other people's information for new business purposes.

'Deep links' are links to specific pages within a larger website, bypassing the 'home page' URL that was long considered the usual entrée to a site. But those days have gone, and visitors to almost any site can now find the home page if they want it. Any competent website designer makes it very clear which entity owns the larger site and its material on every subsidiary page once you get there.

Actually reproducing the complete works of others is another matter, and several bloggers have been pursued in recent years for running copies of whole articles and photographs on their sites. It has become a mini-industry and even a business model for one company—the US-based Righthaven, mentioned in the Introduction—which sued about 275 bloggers and websites that had reproduced material from the newspaper groups it represented. As *Wired* reported, the 'copyright troll' was facing financial ruin after courts had started denying its claims and had awarded costs against it.[12] But it looked unlikely that the scores of small-time bloggers and businesses that had already settled with Righthaven in earlier actions would get any refunds on their substantial damages payouts.

▶ Moral rights: taking the high ground

International conventions and the laws of many countries grant you 'moral rights' over your work in addition to your actionable economic rights. They give you the right to claim authorship of your work through attribution and also the right to object to any changes others might make to your work that might damage your integrity as the creator.

Even if you transferred the copyright in your work to someone else—as you might have done as a freelance blogger or if you were writing as an employee in a government or media organisation—you would still retain your moral rights as an author. This means you can take action against those who might put their own names to your work—or those who have put your name to the work but have changed it to your disadvantage. It operates in part to protect you from unfair attacks and parodies in which your work has been mutilated, distorted beyond recognition or reproduced in a thoroughly inappropriate context that damages your honour.

It won't protect 'reasonable' criticism of your work or any critique you have agreed to. It also does not prevent employers or clients leaving your name off work if you have contracted to allow them to do so. But it sends a warning to others that they shouldn't mess with your work or republish it without giving you due credit. As a blogger, it also means you should be careful when writing parodies pretending to be someone else or denigrating their content and style by chopping and changing it to your satirical ends.

▶ Warning on celebrities: handle carefully

This raises copyright issues for the blogger or social media user writing under the name of someone famous—beyond the hazards we considered earlier in this book.

Many parts of the world have limitations on how you can use the name and image of others, particularly if you are making a profit out of it. These are often called 'personality rights'.

In European and other civil law jurisdictions, there are tough limits on how you can use the likenesses of others—all bundled up in the laws of privacy. You can't just cut and paste someone's photo from the Internet and use it on your blog—especially if it appears to be endorsing your enterprise in some way.

In common law countries such as Australia and the UK, there is an action called 'passing off' that can be launched against you if you have improperly used someone's name or likeness to imply they have entered into some commercial arrangement to endorse your product or service in some way. In its basic form, it offers simple protection to businesses against those who pretend to have some connection with them or endorsement from them. It has been extended in the creative arts to protect newspaper columnists from deceptive parodies of their work being published under their names in competing publications and also to prevent the pen-names of authors being used by their former employers after they have moved on to another title.

The US offers a property right known as the 'right to publicity', and several states have passed laws to extend its basic common law protections. It gives people the right to protect their name, image and other identifying features against commercial exploitation by others. However, like so many areas of US law, it is limited by the First Amendment, so it usually only encompasses blatant cases of exploitation that lack a free expression rationale.

▶ Cybersquatting in your precious domain

Since the advent of the Internet, profiteers have tried to exploit the registration of domain names of unwitting celebrities, businesses and organisations. Lawmakers are still trying to work out how to deal with this problem, and quite often there is absolutely nothing the courts can do because the offender lives in a different jurisdiction. Disputes often end up in the hands of international and national domain registration agencies, which engage in arbitration between the parties to try to resolve the argument over who is really entitled to the name. The Internet Corporation for Assigned Names and Numbers (ICANN) will work with national bodies to withdraw a domain name from a cybersquatter.

It is in your best interests as a blogger to keep a close eye on your domain name registration and to register in advance any close wording variants, especially if you are using your blog to any commercial ends. You never actually 'own' your URL—you are only licensed to use it for a certain period by the registration body. Cybersquatters keep a close eye on the registration process and pounce once a popular name becomes available. They then might use it for selling advertising, stealing your identity or trying to sell the URL licence back to you at an inflated price.

You can't register every possible variation on the spelling of your name, so some spyware and phishing operators register common misspellings of the URLs of famous people and corporations—a practice known as 'typosquatting'.

Even trademark law is inconsistent in the area of domain names, and courts will often not grant relief unless someone clearly demonstrates an intent in bad faith to profit from the deception within the same jurisdiction as the victim.

The international dispute-resolution processes for domain names might be less expensive than litigation, but they can still be beyond the means of the ordinary blogger or small business. WIPO's Arbitration and Mediation Center charges between US$1500 and US$5000 for its services, depending how many domain names are contested and the number of independent panellists needed for the adjudication. It claims it can process such claims within two months of filing. The domain name cases it has handled feature many of the world's leading brands winning URL registration back from shysters and spammers from remote corners of the planet.[13]

▶ **Self-regulation by sites and hosts**

Major social media networks and blog hosts such as Facebook and WordPress also have rules to deter you from registering under other people's or corporations' names. They claim they will act to shut down the offender's account if the target person or organisation complains. But they are sometimes slow to respond and complaints get lost in their bureaucracies. In 2011, PBS reported on the difficulties a Georgia mother faced removing a fake Facebook profile about her thirteen-year-old daughter.[14] This was despite the social network's Statement of Rights and Responsibilities requiring users to use their real names and not 'create an account for anyone other than yourself without permission'. On the other hand, Twitter tolerates numerous impersonation 'handles' set up for comedic purposes. Its policy allows users 'to create parody, commentary, or fan accounts'.

▶ Trademarks: why a Bandaid® solution isn't allowed

Another area of intellectual property of relevance to bloggers and social media users is trademark law. In our globalised commercial world, the wrongful use of a company's name is of special concern to multinational corporations. Many company names have become so commonly used that they have morphed within the language to mean a generic type of product or process rather than the specific brand. The US magazine *Columbia Journalism Review* often runs ads from major companies and the International Trademark Association (INTA) to warn against the misuse of brand names. Examples are the word 'Velcro' being used instead of 'separable fasteners', 'Ray-Ban' in place of 'sunglasses' and 'iTunes' instead of 'audio data computer software'. The INTA has a trademark checklist to help bloggers and other writers avoid infringement.[15] In the end, it's really quite simple: select your words carefully and only use a brand name if you have done your research and are referring to that specific brand intentionally. If not, look to the more descriptive expression for that class of product, service or phenomenon.

Sometimes companies can seem way too protective of their brands, however. In 2011, Facebook failed in its attempt to stop a professional networking start-up for educators using the name 'Teachbook' because the new service was not aimed at Facebook's home jurisdiction of California.[16]

▶ Losing your job over that blog

There can also be legal consequences of your blogging or social media use in the workplace. We don't have the space to go through the gamut of corporations and labour laws here, but there are many examples of employees being fired or disciplined for their inappropriate postings—both at work and at home. Bloggers have criticised their employers' policies in their posts, workers have tweeted about their sporting exploits when on sick leave from the office, while others have made derogatory remarks about their bosses on Facebook pages. In July 2010, the *Huffington Post* ran case studies of thirteen employees who had been fired over their Facebook antics.[17]

▶ Disclosing your sponsors

Trade practices and advertising laws in most countries place obligations on the media to distinguish paid advertising and promotional material from their independent analysis, reviews and news content. 'Misleading and deceptive conduct' provisions mean that those pretending to give unbiased and independent advice can be fined if they are found to be taking secret commissions in return for their endorsements. The US Federal Trade Commission has extended this principle to bloggers who parade as independent reviewers while really being paid for their endorsements. It issued the following warning in 2009:

The post of a blogger who receives cash or in-kind payment to review a product is considered an endorsement. Thus, bloggers who make an endorsement must disclose the material connections they share with the seller of the product or service.[18]

IP expert Christopher Dolan gave three examples on insidecounsel.com of FTC investigations into breaches, including a case in which fashion bloggers failed to reveal they had received gift vouchers from an apparel retailer before they wrote glowing reviews of their clothing range.[19]

IN BRIEF: INTELLECTUAL PROPERTY

- Your form of expression can be protected by copyright, but not your ideas.

- IP laws limit your right to reproduce the work of others; they also protect you if others try to steal your creative output.

- Investigate your local copyright laws so you can take advantage of free use, fair use and fair dealing provisions.

- Give due credit and respect to the creative work of others. Full attribution won't give you immunity from copyright action, but it's sound ethical practice and a good start.

- If you think your own work has been lifted by others, by all means seek advice on your options, but remember that legal action can be complex and expensive.

- Avoid using trademark terms generically. Only use them if you are referring to that specific product.

- Misrepresenting someone's work can breach their moral rights, and setting up fake accounts in their name, impersonating them or 'passing off' your relationship for commercial gain might land you in court.

- Renew your domain name registration regularly or it might be poached by cybersquatters.

- Create a firewall between your private and professional social media usage if you want to retain your job and your professional reputation.

- Always disclose any rewards or incentives you have received from a sponsor. If you receive sponsorship, do not pretend you are offering an independent endorsement of your sponsor's product or service.

CHAPTER 9

BIG BROTHER AND YOU: CENSORSHIP HOTSPOTS AND SECURITY LAWS

#Twitbrief: Free speech is not absolute and First Amendment doesn't travel. Take extra care in some countries. Avoid 'terrorble' jokes. #security

Some describe blogger Gopalan Nair as a principled and fearless dissident, while to others he is a reckless troublemaker. The Singapore-born, US-based attorney spent sixty days in prison in the tiny south-east Asian nation for criticising a judge on his blog in 2008. He described the judge as running a 'kangaroo court' and of 'prostituting herself during the entire proceedings by being nothing more than an employee of Mr Lee Kuan Yew and his son and carrying out their orders'. The words breached section 228 of the nation's penal code, which bans the insulting of a judicial officer. His arrest was condemned internationally by free expression activists, including Reporters Without Borders. Back in the sanctuary of the US after his release, Nair returned to his blog to thumb his nose at the Singaporean court.

> . . . I am defying the undertaking that I gave in court on September 12, 2008 when I admitted being in contempt of court . . . I had also given an undertaking to remove the 2 blog posts, of Sept 1 2008 and Sept 6, 2008 which referred to my trial and conviction before Judge James Leong in the Subordinate Courts for disorderly behaviour and insulting a policeman, charges entirely made up by the police to discredit me. I will be re-posting those 2 blog posts and stand by every word that I had written in them . . .[1]

Nair was struck off the roll of advocates and solicitors of Singapore in 2011, but remains a practising lawyer in California and continues haranguing the island's government and judiciary from afar on his Singapore Dissident blog.

▶ The First Amendment doesn't have a passport

Bloggers such as Gopalan Nair from countries like the US that have a well-developed right to free expression find the censorship of many other nations abhorrent. Yet if you decide to defy their regulations openly, you may face the same fate as Nair—a prison term.

It might only be forty five words long, but if you're an American cyberjournalist, blogger or social media user, you can't pack the First Amendment in your luggage when you travel abroad. The famous clause protecting the press and free speech does not travel well when your Web 2.0 material is viewed in foreign lands.

That shouldn't worry you if you have published within US law and are happy to sit at home in North Dakota or Hawaii, tapping away on the device of your choice. But you should think twice before stepping onto an aircraft and touching down in a jurisdiction where there are tougher gags on free expression. Of course, citizens from the US and other countries with higher levels of free expression—such as Scandinavia, Canada, the UK and New Zealand—don't have *carte blanche* at home, either. Even those countries draw the line at criminal publications involving prohibited materials, such as child pornography, or engaging in criminal activity, such as fraud or terrorism.

But there are many things you can happily publish on social media or on blogs in western democracies that might trigger lawsuits, harsh fines or jail terms in some countries.

▶ Enemies of the state

You might call yourself a blogger, a citizen journalist, a tweeter or even just a Facebook friend, but in some countries you are an enemy of the state. You have the right to remain silent. That's about the only right you do have in some places—and you would be well advised to exercise it well in advance if you plan to visit any of them.

The flip side of free expression is censorship. Lawyers call this 'prior restraint' by governments. The greatest censors are countries that allow their judges and politicians to exercise prior restraint on writers and broadcasters. The centuries-old rule against prior restraint originated in the British courts, and it means the courts in western democracies should not intervene to stop your posting unless it is a very serious breach. Countries with a high level of free expression would prefer to deal with any problem your words have created after publication rather than restraining them prior to publication. Of course, there are many exceptions to this rule.

▶ **Bloggers' freedom**

Debate over your right to blog or express yourself in social media postings happens in the parliaments and courtrooms of societies in which free expression is a valued concept. Sadly, in many countries that debate is not even allowed to occur. It is also disappointing that there is no enforceable worldwide agreement on free expression as a fundamental human right, although some nations and regions have managed to entrench free expression into their constitutions, with mixed impact.

The key international document is the United Nations' Universal Declaration of Human Rights, which in 1948 enshrined free expression at Article 19: 'Everyone has the right to freedom of opinion and expression; this right includes freedom to hold opinions without interference and to seek, receive and impart information and ideas through any media regardless of frontiers.'[2]

At face value, this statement seems to give all the world's citizens a right to free expression. But it was only ever meant to be a declaration of a lofty goal and has many limitations.

Stronger protections came internationally in 1966, when the UN adopted the International Covenant on Civil and Political Rights, prompting a series of binding treaties. The covenant introduces a right to free expression for the world's citizens, again at Article 19: 'Everyone shall have the right to freedom of expression; this right shall include freedom to seek, receive and impart information and ideas of all kinds, regardless of frontiers, either orally, in writing or in print, in the form of art, or through any other media of his choice.'

It sounds like it was written for bloggers and social media users. However, the right is limited because the covenant imposes special duties for the respect of the rights and reputations of others, and for the protection of national security, public order, public health and morals. Add to this the fact that many countries have not ratified the covenant and you are left without much real protection at this level. Complaints about individual countries' breaches can be brought to the Office of the High Commissioner for Human Rights, but the process can take several years and is often not resolved, as its annual reports demonstrate.

A positive of the UN right was that it fed through into regional conventions, and then into the laws of their nations. Rights charters exist in Africa, the Americas and Europe, and free expression or a free press is guaranteed by the constitutions of many countries internationally.

United States

The starting point for any examination of free expression is almost always the First Amendment to the US Constitution. The famous fourteen-word portion protecting free expression in the US states is: 'Congress shall make no law . . . abridging the freedom of speech, or of the press.' The US Supreme Court has applied a broad interpretation of those words to an array of writing and publishing scenarios.[3] It has been held to cover the gamut of writing you would do as a blogger or social media user, especially if you are addressing a matter of genuine public concern. But even in the US the First Amendment protections are sometimes not enough. In 2006 two bloggers were jailed. As we saw in Chapter 6, video activist and blogger Josh Wolf spent seven-and-a-half months in prison for refusing, during an arson trial, to hand over some footage of protesters he had posted to his site.[4] Indian graduate student Vikram S. Buddhi served four years for allegedly posting death threats against former president George W. Bush on his website.[5]

In 2011 the US government successfully petitioned the District Court of Virginia to force Twitter to hand over account information about five people related to its WikiLeaks investigations, including the site's founder, Julian Assange, and the soldier accused of leaking classified documents. The court held that neither First Amendment free association arguments nor Fourth Amendment privacy arguments could prevent the release of the data to the authorities.[6]

Europe

The European Convention on Human Rights has had a strong impact on the laws of countries on that continent. Free expression is protected in Article 10 and it carries similar responsibilities to those in the Universal Declaration of Human Rights. The difference is that free expression has been built into the judicial and legislative systems of European countries via the Council of Europe and the European Union. Several human rights cases have challenged decisions in the various countries, resulting in the local courts being challenged in the European Court of Human Rights. This has happened in several free expression and Internet cases, which have mainly concerned privacy law.[7]

European countries vary greatly in their levels of free expression. In 2010 they occupied sixteen of the top twenty places in the Reporters Without Borders World Press Freedom Index.[8] But some—like Russia, Belarus and Montenegro—did not even make the top 100 countries on that list. The highest levels of free expression are in Scandinavia, with Finland, Iceland, Norway and Sweden sharing the highest ranking with Switzerland and the Netherlands.

United Kingdom

Notions of free expression have been entrenched in British philosophy, law and politics for several centuries, but only at the end of the last century was free expression set in binding legislation as a human right. The UK imported it from Article 10 of the European Convention of Human Rights when it passed its *Human Rights Act* in 1998. At that point, many of its court decisions related to free expression started to deviate from those of its former colonies, particularly in relation to the balance of free speech and privacy.

A series of privacy decisions related to celebrities has developed over the past twenty years and has resulted in a whole new privacy law in the UK, where there was previously little precedent. In 2011 the motor-racing entrepreneur Max Mosley went to the European Court of Human Rights to have British laws changed so that the media would have to advise a celebrity before revealing private details about them.[9] Despite winning a privacy action against the *News of the World* newspaper in the

British courts (discussed in Chapter 5), he was still seething over aspects of his sex life being falsely reported on the front page in 2008. This was his attempt to have the privacy right at Article 8 in the European Convention read as superior to the free expression right at Article 10. He failed, which offers some hope to bloggers and social media users that privacy will not trump free expression when genuine matters of public concern are at stake.

The Commonwealth

Internet writers will find that standards of free expression vary considerably among countries that were former British colonies and are now members of the Commonwealth. They have a shared legal heritage in the case law of England—known as the 'common law'—but their free speech positions are often shaped by their own constitutions and the decisions of their courts since nationhood. Their rankings on the World Press Freedom Index in 2010 ranged from New Zealand at number 8 through to Rwanda at number 169.

Most Commonwealth constitutions, including those of Canada, India and Papua New Guinea, guarantee freedom of expression.[10] Such a freedom is not stated explicitly in the Constitution of Australia, but its High Court has ruled that there is an 'implied right' to free expression on matters of government and politics in its constitution.[11] New Zealand's Bill of Rights, enacted in 1990, states at section 14: 'Everyone has the right to freedom of expression, including the freedom to seek, receive, and impart information and opinions of any kind in any form.' In 2011 the NZ Supreme Court found that this right even protected Valerie Morse, an anti-war protester who burned her country's flag during a dawn memorial service in Wellington.[12] Her conviction for offensive behaviour was set aside. That's quite a strong signal to Kiwi bloggers that online political criticism will be tolerated, at least in their own country.

Other countries

Sadly, that is not the case in many other nations. The only country outside the US, Europe and the Commonwealth to rank highly in free expression rankings over recent years has been Japan. Despite having regional charters of human rights, several countries in Africa and Central and South America have shown little respect for Internet or media freedom. The so-called 'Twitter revolutions' throughout the Middle East and North Africa in 2010 and 2011 showed how social media could help accelerate movements striving for better human rights. But despite the impact of 'people power' in such countries, there is still evidence of censorship and intimidation throughout much of the world. No regional human rights convention exists in Asia, and the Hong Kong-based Asian Human Rights Commission provides an ongoing chronicle of abuses, many involving the gagging of journalists, bloggers and dissidents.

The countries of the world with the highest levels of censorship maintain tight control over expression and take firm action against online writers who use the Internet to question their governments' authority. These are places where you get labelled a dissident and face jail if you blog or tweet to express your political views. Reporters Without Borders has released a list of enemies of free Internet speech: Burma, China, Cuba, Iran, North Korea, Saudi

Arabia, Syria, Turkmenistan, Uzbekistan and Vietnam. They are countries where bloggers, journalists and other dissidents have been imprisoned or tortured for daring to write what they think or for encouraging others to do so. (Yale law student Nate Blevins devised a superb infographic for showing the extent of cyber-censorship, posted at yalelawtech.org in May 2011.[13])

Governments in such countries block access to full Internet use via systems such as the 'Great Firewall of China'. While the Internet is seen by many as a wonderful new tool for democracy, there is a downside to the use of social media and blogs if your nation does not value free speech: your web-based activities can be monitored quite easily by security forces, and your careless use of such media can leave you dangerously exposed. Blogger Nay Phone Latt served four years in a Burmese jail for reporting in his blog about the unfolding demonstrations against the government in Rangoon in 2007, and for describing how hard it was for young Burmese to express themselves freely.[14] Chinese blogger Ran Yunfei was among several arrested in a crackdown on dissent by government authorities in 2011. He spent six months in prison and was released on the condition he did not speak with the media or continue to share his political views online.[15]

Repressive regimes also engage in modern propaganda techniques, such as cyberattacks on target websites and 'phishing' for dissident password information to access their email addresses and other contact details.[16] The US has declared cyberspace the new 'fifth sphere of war', after land, air, sea and space.[17]

▶ **God save the King**

Some countries have laws making it an offence to insult the royal family, with Thailand, a nation with an otherwise free and vibrant media, the most active in its use. It is called 'lese-majesty', and in that country it can carry a maximum jail term of fifteen years. Authorities have charged as many as 100 people a year with the offence in recent years, with several unsuspecting foreigners languishing in jail because of their published criticisms of royalty. Colorado resident Joe Gordon was detained for eighty-four days in Thailand in 2011 on a charge of translating an unauthorised biography critical of the king.[18] This came just three years after Australian Harry Nicolaides spent six months in prison over a passage offensive to the Crown Prince that appeared in his self-published novel. The book only sold a few copies, although extracts had been published on a US-based website. Nicolaides wrote in the *Monthly* of his traumatic stay in an overcrowded 'Bangkok Hilton', as he tried to navigate court appearances and brief lawyers and diplomats trying to negotiate his freedom. Thailand should appear high on the travel warning list for bloggers.

It is not alone. Other nations have the lese-majesty laws or equivalents. As we saw in Chapter 4, journalist Bashar Al-Sayegh spent three days in jail in 2007 because someone else had posted an insulting comment about the Emir of Kuwait on his website. Brunei, Denmark, the Netherlands, Spain and Morocco also have the lese-majesty laws and each has used them to prosecute insults to their royal families in recent years. Poland, Germany, Switzerland, the Maldives, Egypt, Syria, Kazakhstan, Belarus, Zimbabwe and Greece have crimes related to the defamation of heads of state of foreign countries or their own. They have been used several times this century.[19]

▶ Your rights in action

How does all this affect what you can or cannot write online? The right to remain silent might be your safest option, but bloggers and social media users feel compelled to have their voices heard. It offers some comfort to be publishing from a country that has constitutional safeguards for free expression and ranks highly in world media freedom listings. You also need to be extra careful that your words or images do not implicate someone in a country with a stronger censorship regime than your own. Remember, your blogs, tweets and Facebook pages can be accessed by authorities in other countries, even if they have an Internet firewall in place for their citizens. Also, you need to be careful when you write about the activities of your friends and colleagues from other countries. I'm sure you wouldn't want another blogger's imprisonment or torture on your conscience if the security agencies in their home country arrest them over something you have have posted from the safety of your free expression haven. You need to bear this in mind if your network extends to vulnerable individuals living in such regimes.

▶ Plan your travel itinerary carefully

So, what does all this mean for the average western cyberjournalist, blogger or microblogger? Quite simply: think before you publish, and think before you travel.

You won't be extradited and tried by aliens if you keep within the laws of your own country. But you should revise your travel itinerary to avoid countries whose governments or citizens may have been offended by your blogs or postings.

If you're an American citizen who has been particularly provocative in your writing and you really must travel, then consider your other fifty-five US state and territory jurisdictions, or perhaps pack your bags for a Scandinavian vacation. While they don't have a First Amendment, those countries usually come in well ahead of the US on the Freedom House and Reporters Without Borders free expression rankings.

▶ Terror is no laughing matter

Twitter and Facebook are great outlets for one-liners and satire, but police and security agencies are not known for their sense of humour. Twenty-seven-year-old trainee accountant Paul Chambers learned that the hard way when he was arrested on UK terrorism charges for jokingly tweeting a threat to blow up a British airport.[20] Air traffic was delayed by a heavy snowfall and Chambers was desperate to visit a female friend in Northern Ireland, so he light-heartedly tweeted to her and his 650 followers: 'Robin Hood Airport closed. You have got a week to get your s— together, otherwise I'm blowing the airport sky high!' Police swooped a week later and he was questioned on the terrorism charges before being convicted and fined £1000 on a lesser charge of causing nuisance. He planned an appeal to the High Court.

Across the English Channel, twenty-three-year-old unemployed Frenchman François Cousteix was surprised one evening to find French police and US FBI agents at his front door. Operating under the name 'Hacker Croll', he had made it his hobby to hack into celebrities' social media accounts for fun. He had accessed the social media account of celebrity Britney Spears but came to the attention of international security agencies when he hacked into the Twitter account of US President Barack Obama. He escaped with a five-month parole sentence.[21]

There is a simple lesson from these cases: do not joke about national security matters.

▶ National security and anti-terrorism laws post 9/11

Governments throughout the world ramped up their national security laws in the wake of the terrorist attacks on the US in September 2001. Even in countries with a high regard for civil liberties and free expression, new powers were handed to security agencies and police to aid in the detection and arrest of suspected terrorists. Pressure mounted in western democracies for even tougher laws after the Bali bombings in 2002 and 2005 and the 7/7 London attacks in 2005.[22]

Publishing restrictions in the name of national security existed long before 9/11. Sedition and treason offences for encouraging public unrest, violence or the overthrow of rulers date back to feudal times, when governments tried to enforce loyalty upon ordinary citizens. While many countries have phased out these ancient crimes, such laws are still used in some places as mechanisms for intimidation and repression. Anti-terrorism laws were also used in western democracies prior to 2001. The UK passed special laws to respond to Irish Republican Army terrorism throughout the twentieth century, while New Zealand introduced new restrictions after the French bombing of the Greenpeace ship *Rainbow Warrior* in 1985.

But the early twenty-first-century attacks on the west triggered a wave of new anti-terror laws that would affect the free expression of journalists and Internet users. A glance at the Australian Parliamentary Library's Terrorism Law directory shows hundreds of anti-terror laws introduced in the first decade of the twenty-first century under the banner of the so-called 'War on Terror'.[23]

America led the way with its *USA PATRIOT Act* of 2001: the title stands for 'Uniting (and) Strengthening America (by) Providing Appropriate Tools Required (to) Intercept (and) Obstruct Terrorism'.[24] President Obama's administration extended the legislation for a further four years from 2011.

Other nations followed suit after 9/11, including the UK, Canada, Australia and New Zealand. Ottawa software developer Momin Khawaja became the first person charged under Canada's anti-terror laws, but in 2011 challenged his conviction on constitutional grounds.[25] In Australia, Belal Saadalah Khazaal was sentenced to twelve years in jail in 2009 for 'making a document connected with assistance in a terrorist act' after he created an ebook titled 'Provisions on the Rules of Jihad', which allegedly targeted foreign governments and leaders. He won the right to a retrial after an appeal in 2011.[26]

There have been too many anti-terror laws introduced internationally to detail here, but some may affect you if you are a cyberjournalist or blogger. They include:

- increased surveillance powers for spy agencies and police
- new detention and questioning regimes
- seizure of notes and computer archives
- exposing confidential sources to identification

- closing certain court proceedings so they are unreportable
- exposing bloggers to fines and jail if you report on some anti-terror operations
- making it an offence to merely 'associate' or 'communicate' with those suspected of security crimes
- exposing bloggers and social media users to criminal charges if you publish anything seen as inciting terrorism.

Governments also go straight to search engines and ISPs and demand they remove material; as Google's Transparency Reports document, these companies often comply.[27] But some have complained that Google and YouTube have not responded quickly enough when asked to take down terrorist material. Burst.net certainly acted fast when the FBI advised it that some blogs it hosted on the free blogetery.com site contained terrorist material suspected of being used by al-Qaeda. It shut the site down, along with the 70,000 blogs it hosted.[28] Blogetery resurfaced a month later with a different host.

The United Nations introduced a range of protocols suggesting that countries adopt minimum standards for combating terrorism. A Mexican radio commentator and a maths tutor were jailed and faced a maximum thirty-year prison sentence in 2011 on terrorism and sabotage charges after they tweeted false reports that gunmen were attacking schools in the city of Veracruz.[29] The misinformation prompted parents to panic, and some were involved in motor accidents as they rushed to fetch their children. 'Here, there were twenty-six car accidents, or people left their cars in the middle of the streets to run and pick up their children, because they thought these things were occurring at their kids' schools,' an official told Associated Press.[30] The false reports followed weeks of gangland violence in the city.

'My sister-in-law just called me all upset, they just kidnapped five children from the school,' tutor Gilberto Martinez Vera allegedly tweeted. He followed that message with: 'I don't know what time it happened, but it's true.' The other accused had retweeted the false reports to her followers. Amnesty International called the arrest an affront to free expression, while a media academic described the tweeting as a poor use of the medium, but not deserving of terrorism charges.[31]

IN BRIEF: CENSORSHIP AND SECURITY

- Be cautious when blogging or using social media to discuss politics in another country or national security at home.

- Get familiar with your rights at a national and international level, but understand that free expression is often trumped by other rights and interests.

- Take special care when discussing the internal affairs of another regime from the sanctuary of a 'safe' western democracy. You might be in danger if you ever decide to travel there, and you might place dissidents in danger if you mention them in your postings.

- Join or follow international free expression groups, such as the Electronic Frontier Foundation, Amnesty International, Reporters Without Borders, Freedom House and IFEX, and help raise awareness of free Internet expression.

- Note the particularly tough laws controlling criticism of royalty in some countries, especially Thailand.

- Before you travel, look carefully at the censorship record of the nations you plan to visit and ensure you have not published anything online that might put you in breach of their laws.

- Never joke about terrorism. Others have served jail time for doing so.

READ ALL ABOUT IT!

Twitbrief: Useful free expression and legal resources for the serious blogger and social media user. #ngos #references #lobbyists #tweeps #medialaw

This book has a modest aim: to offer the serious blogger and social media user an introduction to the main areas of law you might encounter in your writing.

Some of you might want to research all or any of these topics further, or to engage with some of the experts in the field for further information or support. Here are some of the valuable resources and individuals I turn to for information on this rapidly changing field.

Free expression non-government organisations
Committee to Protect Journalists (New York, NY, USA)
Promotes press freedom worldwide by defending the rights of journalists.
Web: www.cpj.org
Facebook: www.facebook.com/committeetoprotectjournalists
Twitter: @pressfreedom

Electronic Frontier Foundation (San Francisco, CA, USA)
Fights for free expression, mainly in the courts, bringing and defending lawsuits.
Web: www.eff.org
Facebook: www.facebook.com/eff
Twitter: @EFF

First Amendment Center (Nashville, TN, USA)
Works to preserve and protect First Amendment freedoms.
Web: www.firstamendmentcenter.org
Facebook: www.facebook.com/firstamendmentcenter
Twitter: @1stAmendmentCtr

International Center For Journalists (Washington, DC, USA)
Promotes quality journalism and an independent, vigorous media worldwide.
Web: www.icfj.org
Facebook: www.facebook.com/icfj.org
Twitter: @ICFJ

International Press Institute (Vienna, Austria)
Global network of editors, media executives and leading journalists dedicated to free expression.
Web: www.freemedia.at
Facebook: www.facebook.com/InternationalPressInstituteIPI
Twitter: @globalfreemedia

Reporters sans Frontières/Reporters Without Borders (Paris, France)
Promotes and defends free expression of journalists, bloggers and cyber-dissidents.
Web: en.rsf.org
Facebook: www.facebook.com/Reporterssansfrontieres
Twitter: @RSF_RWB

The Reporters Committee for Freedom of the Press
(Arlington, VA, USA)
Provides free legal assistance to journalists and fights
court orders demanding the disclosure of sources.
Web: www.rcfp.org/index.php
Twitter: @rcfp

Social media law and media law lobbyists and research centres

International Forum for Responsible Media
Collaborative expert blog debating issues of media
responsibility.
Web: inforrm.wordpress.com/about
Facebook: www.facebook.com/pages/Inforrm/150817531638899
Twitter: @INFORRM

Berkman Center for Internet and Society
(Harvard Law School, Cambridge, MA, USA)
Aims to understand cyberspace and assess the need for
laws and sanctions.
Web: cyber.law.harvard.edu
Facebook: www.facebook.com/BerkmanCenter
Twitter: @berkmancenter

Citizen Media Law Project
(Harvard Law School, Cambridge, MA, USA)
Researches and provides legal help, education and
resources for online and citizen media.
Web: www.citmedialaw.org
Facebook: www.facebook.com/pages/
    Citizen-Media-Law-Project/93319708219
Twitter: @citmedialaw

International Media Lawyers Association (Oxford, UK)
Maintains a database covering media law, media freedom and media policy in more than 20 countries.
Web: www.internationalmedialawyers.org

Suffolk Media Law (Boston, MA, USA)
Suffolk University Law School student organisation covering communications law and media policy.
Web: suffolkmedialaw.com
Facebook: www.facebook.com/pages/
    Suffolk-Media-Law/118072541553518
Twitter: @SuffolkMediaLaw

Legal sites

Australasian Legal Information Institute (Sydney, Australia)
Australasian legal materials.
Web: www.austlii.edu.au
Facebook: www.facebook.com/pages/AustLII/142416019103348
Twitter: @austlii

British and Irish Legal Information Institute (London, UK)
British and Irish primary legal materials.
Web: www.bailii.org

Canadian Legal Information Institute (Ontario, Canada)
Legal documents from Canada's federal, provincial and territorial governments.
Web: www.canlii.org
Facebook: www.facebook.com/CanLII.org
Twitter: @CanLII

Justia.com (California, USA)
Free US case law, codes, regulations, legal articles, legal blog databases.
Web: www.justia.com
Facebook: www.facebook.com/justia
Twitter: @justiacom

Leagle, Inc. (Washington, DC, USA)
Primary case law from all US federal courts and all state higher courts.
Web: www.leagle.com
Facebook: www.facebook.com/pages/Leagle/393868331208
Twitter: @LeagleBriefs

Legalis.net (France)
Case law and technology law news from France.
Web: www.legalis.net
Facebook: www.facebook.com/Legalis.net
Twitter: @legalisnet

Parliament of Australia (Canberra, Australia)
Australian Parliamentary Hansards, Bills, etc.
Web: www.aph.gov.au

The Gazette of Law and Journalism (Sydney, Australia)
Covers Australian court cases, legislation and policy issues that affect the media. Paywall.
Web: www.glj.com.au

World Legal Information Institute (Sydney, Australia)
International legal database.
Web: www.worldlii.org

Social media 'blawgers' (law bloggers)

Antonin I. Pribetic (Toronto, Canada)
Canadian trial and appellate lawyer.
Web: thetrialwarrior.com
Twitter: @APribetic

David Allen Green (London, UK)
Critical and liberal look at law and policy, with a focus on media law.
Web: www.newstatesman.com/blogs/david-allen-green
Twitter: @DavidAllenGreen

Eoin O'Dell/'cearta.ie' (Ireland)
Irish perspective on 'cearta' (rights) covering free expression, media, IT and cyber law.
Web: www.cearta.ie
Twitter: @cearta

Rick Shera/'l@w.geek.nz' (New Zealand)
New Zealand ICT, IP blogging on Kiwi Internet and media law.
Web: lawgeeknz.posterous.com
Twitter: @lawgeeknz

Sheldon Toplitt/'The Unruly of Law' Blawg (USA)
Attorney and writer/editor who comments on social media law and media law.
Web: theunrulyoflaw.blogspot.com
Twitter: @theunrulyoflaw

Social media law tweeps

Clancco: Art and Law (USA)
Official feed on art law. Copyright, trademark, moral rights, deaccessioning, free speech.
Twitter: @Clancco_ArtLaw

Craig Moore (USA)
American social media law attorney.
Twitter: @CraigGMoore

Entertainment Law (USA)
Producer of entertainment law podcast.
Twitter: @entlawupdate

Evan Brown (USA)
Technology lawyer, blogger, thinker and regular on 'This Week in Law' (TWiL)
Web: twit.tv/twil
Twitter: @Internetcases

Evgeny Morozov (USA)
Author of The Net Delusion: The Dark Side of Internet Freedom.
Twitter: @evgenymorozov

IP Law Updates (International)
Commentary, analysis and alerts from leading IP lawyers and law firms.
Twitter: @IPLawAlerts

Joshua Rozenberg (UK)
Britain's best-known commentator on the law.
Twitter: @JoshuaRozenberg

Judith Townend—'Meeja Law' (UK)
Media law and ethics for online publishers, with useful links.
Web: meejalaw.com
Twitter: @meejalaw and @JTownend

Justin Silverman (USA)
Founding president of Suffolk Media Law and board member of New England First Amendment Center.
Twitter: @JustinSilverman

Kate Sutherland (Canada)
Professor who researches defamation and writers' lawsuits.
Twitter: @LawandLit

Kay Lam-MacLeod (Australia)
IT lawyer who comments on social media law.
Twitter: @IDEALAW

Kyu Yu Houm (Oregon, USA)
Media law professor at University of Oregon.
Twitter: @MarshallYoum

Leanne O'Donnell (Australia)
Lawyer and freelance writer on social media law.
Twitter: @MsLods

Mark Pearson (Australia)
Twitter feed on media and social media law and free expression from the author of this book.
Twitter: @journlaw

Media Guardian (UK)
Official Twitter feed for MediaGuardian.co.uk updates.
Twitter: @mediaguardian

Melissa Castan (Australia)
Law lecturer who tweets on law and media.
Twitter: @MsCastan

PrivacyMemes (International)
'The pulse of online privacy'—an interesting source of privacy news.
Twitter: @PrivacyMemes

Social Media Law (USA)
Commentary on social media and the law.
Twitter: @SMediaLaw

The FreeSpeech Daily (International)
Daily news on violations of the right to free speech from around the world.
Twitter: @FreeSpeechDaily

Theodore Konstantakopoulos (Greece)
Information technology/intellectual property and privacy lawyer.
Twitter: @CyberspaceLaw

Media law / Internet law books

Browning, John G. (2010) *The lawyer's guide to social networking: Understanding social media's impact on the law.* Boston: Aspatore.

Burrows, John & Cheer, Ursula (2010) *Media law in New Zealand*, 6th edn. Wellington: LexisNexis NZ.

Castendyk, Oliver & Dommering, Egbert & Scheuer, Alexander (2008) *European media law.* The Netherlands: Kluwer Law International.

Collins, Matthew (2010) *The law of defamation and the Internet*, 3rd edn. New York: Oxford University Press.

Crook, Tim (2010) *Comparative media law and ethics*. Oxon: Routledge.

Goldberg, David & Sutter, Gavin & Walden, Ian (2009) *Media law and practice*. Oxford: Oxford University Press.

Hamilton, Sheryl N. (2009) *Law's expression: communication, law and media in Canada*. Ontario: LexisNexis.

Jobb, Dean (2011) *Media law for Canadian journalists*, 2nd edn. Toronto: Emond Montgomery Publications.

Packard, Ashley (2010) *Digital media law*. Malden: Wiley-Blackwell.

Pearson, Mark & Polden, Mark (2011) *The journalist's guide to media law*, 4th edn. Crows Nest: Allen & Unwin.

Pember, Don R. & Calvert, Clay (2011) *Mass media law*, 17th edn. New York: McGraw Hill.

Smartt, Ursula (2011) *Media and entertainment law*. Oxon: Routledge.

Sparrow, Andrew Peter (2010) *The law of virtual worlds and Internet social networks*. Surrey: Gower.

Towers-Romero, Sandi (2009) *Media and entertainment law*. Clifton Park: Delmar Cengage Learning.

Wang, Faye Fangfei (2010) *Internet jurisdiction and choice of law: Legal practices in the EU, US and China*. Cambridge: Cambridge University Press.

Weisenhaus, Doreen (2007) *Hong Kong media law: A guide for journalists and media professionals*. Aberdeen: Hong Kong University Press.

NOTES

▶ **Introduction**

1 http://il.findacase.com/research/wfrmDocViewer.aspx/xq/
   fac.20110315_0000663.NIL.htm/qx
2 http://www.vegasinc.com/news/2011/jun/22/
   judge-tosses-righthaven-suit-against-former-prosec/
3 http://www.crikey.com.au/2010/12/03/
   why-editors-rarely-sue-for-defamation/
4 http://www.telegraph.co.uk/technology/facebook/7912731/Law-
   student-wins-10000-after-being-branded-a-paedophile-on-
   Facebook.html
5 http://www.independent.co.uk/news/media/online/30000-twitter-
   users-could-face-legal-action-over-gag-breaches-2287787.html

▶ **Chapter 1**

1 http://www.flickr.com/photos/sesh00/515961023/
2 http://cyber.law.harvard.edu/property00/jurisdiction/zipposum.html
3 http://www.austlii.edu.au/au/cases/cth/HCA/2002/56.html
4 http://www.keytlaw.com/Cases/getaped.htm
5 http://www.transformationsjournal.org/journal/issue_11/article_04.shtml
6 http://en.rsf.org/turquie-youtube-bows-to-pressure-from-03-11-
   2010,38742.html
7 http://www.ifex.org/india/2008/08/26/
   bombay_high_court_orders_google
8 http://www.theaustralian.com.au/national-affairs/behrendt-repents-
   for-twitter-slur-on-black-leader/story-fn59niix-1226039396368

9   http://www.linksandlaw.com/linkingcases-linkstoillegalmaterial.htm
10 http://canlii.ca/en/ca/scc/doc/2011/2011scc47/2011scc47.html
11 http://www.telegraph.co.uk/comment/personal-view/8137164/My-Twitter-row-with-Stephen-Fry.html
12 http://www.minterellison.com/M_20100401_liabilityFor/

▶ **Chapter 2**

1   http://www.citmedialaw.org/threats/simorangkir-v-love
2   http://www.reuters.com/article/2011/05/27/us-courtneylove-idUSTRE74Q6UC20110527
3   http://www.splc.org/news/newsflash.asp?id=2229
4   http://www.citmedialaw.org/threats/banks-v-milum
5   http://www.law.cornell.edu/uscode/html/uscode47/usc_sec_47_00000230----000-.html
6   http://menmedia.co.uk/manchestereveningnews/news/s/208/208821_bloggers_beware_of_libel_trials.html
7   http://www.guardian.co.uk/technology/2011/may/29/twitter-anonymous-user-legal-battle
8   http://canlii.ca/en/ca/scc/doc/2011/2011scc47/2011scc47.html
9   http://www.forbes.com/sites/marcbabej/2011/05/24/daimler-benz-has-a-critical-facebook-page-shut-down/
10 http://suffolkmedialaw.com/2011/07/06/tripadvisor-com-commenter-sued-for-defamation/
11 http://www.firstamendmentcenter.org/judge-dismisses-libel-claim-against-conservative-blogger
12 http://www.lawgazette.co.uk/in-practice/media-law-offers-amends
13 http://www.stephens.com.au/view/8/2010091585857/
14 http://www.usatoday.com/news/nation/2006-10-10-internet-defamation-case_x.htm
15 http://www.guardian.co.uk/books/2008/aug/27/salmanrushdie.law
16 http://decisions.justice.wa.gov.au/supreme/supdcsn.nsf/c04d382e733a94a148256fc4002b2e2b/12ce060858b5eb9e4825641300205ca6?OpenDocument&Highlight=2,rindos
17 http://www.publications.parliament.uk/pa/ld199899/ldjudgmt/jd991028/rey01.htm
18 http://scc.lexum.org/en/2009/2009scc61/2009scc61.html
19 http://defamationlawblog.wordpress.com/2010/01/25/grant-v-torstar-and-the-defence-of-responsible-communication-implications-for-bloggers-and-users-of-other-online-media/
20 http://papers.ssrn.com/sol3/papers.cfm?abstract_id=1664859
21 http://caselaw.lp.findlaw.com/scripts/getcase.pl?navby=case&court=us&vol=376&page=254

22 https://www.eff.org/issues/bloggers/legal/liability/defamation
23 http://www.hri.org/docs/ECHR50.html
24 http://pcmlp.socleg.ox.ac.uk/sites/pcmlp.socleg.ox.ac.uk/files/
   defamationreport.pdf
25 http://www.english.rfi.fr/
   france/20101120-three-fired-facebook-criticisms-bosses
26 http://citation.allacademic.com/meta/p_mla_apa_research_
   citation/1/1/2/2/9/pages112292/p112292-3.php
27 http://coveringchina.org/2011/05/10/
   the-endless-narrative-of-criminal-defamation-in-china/
28 http://news.theage.com.au/breaking-news-technology/china-
   bloggers-fined-for-defamation-report-20091226-lfni.html
29 http://www.nzherald.co.nz/world/news/article.
   cfm?c_id=2&objectid=10730019
30 http://theonlinecitizen.com/2009/08/former-teacher-sues-
   association-of-bloggers-president-and-founder-jayne-goh/
31 http://www.journalismnow.com/news/blog-news/
   vietnam-police-release-gossip-blogger-on-bail
32 http://www.thejakartaglobe.com/home/
   shock-guilty-verdict-in-prita-mulyasari-saga/451797
33 http://mybroadband.co.za/news/internet/6580-man-bust-for-
   facebook-insults.html

▶ Chapter 3

1 http://www.dailymail.co.uk/news/article-2004196/Well-jail-jurors-
   use-Facebook-warns-judge-woman-imprisoned-months.html
2 http://www.guardian.co.uk/technology/2010/dec/14/
   twitter-allowed-bail-hearing
3 http://www.telegraph.co.uk/news/worldnews/wikileaks/8202262/
   WikiLeaks-Julian-Assange-bail-hearing-makes-legal-history-with-
   Twitter-ruling.html
4 http://www.independent.co.uk/news/media/online/twitter-to-be-
   allowed-in-courts-2165032.html
5 http://www.theaustralian.com.au/news/judges-have-final-decision-
   on-twitter/story-e6frgal6-1225788184795
6 http://www.abajournal.com/news/article/
   bloggers_cover_us_trials_of_accused_terrorists_cheney_aide_and_
   iowa_landlor
7 http://www.citmedialaw.org/legal-guide/
   live-blogging-and-tweeting-from-court
8 http://saraganim.files.wordpress.com/2010/10/tweeting-in-court-
   nets-jail-term.pdf

9   http://edition.cnn.com/2008/TECH/04/25/twitter.buck/index.html
10 http://www.guardian.co.uk/uk/2011/apr/19/
    twitter-midlands-magistrates-court
11 http://www.judiciary.gov.uk/Resources/JCO/Documents/Speeches/
    mr-speech-jsb-lecture-march-2011.pdf
12 http://www.echr.coe.int/NR/rdonlyres/D5CC24A7-DC13-4318-
    B457-5C9014916D7A/0/ENG_CONV.pdf
13 http://www.un.org/en/documents/udhr/index.shtml
14 http://www.crikey.com.au/2011/11/04/
    simons-to-tweet-or-not-to-tweet-from-court/
15 http://www.canlii.org/en/ns/nsca/
    doc/2011/2011nsca26/2011nsca26.html
16 http://www.telegraph.co.uk/technology/twitter/8531175/Ryan-Giggs-
    named-as-Premier-League-footballer-in-gagging-order-row.html
17 http://www.telegraph.co.uk/technology/twitter/8530076/Journalist-
    could-be-jailed-over-Twitter-comments-about-injunctions.html
18 http://www.nytimes.com/2008/07/15/technology/15law.html?pagew
    anted=1&ref=technology
19 http://sdfla.blogspot.com/2008/01/gag-order-lifted-in-part.html
20 http://lawpublications.seattleu.edu/sulr/vol32/iss3/8/
21 http://www.washingtonpost.com/blogs/blogpost/post/amanda-knox-
    trial-blogger-silenced-by-google/2011/05/16/AFofFp4G_blog.html
22 http://www.austlii.edu.au/cgi-bin/sinodisp/au/cases/vic/
    VSCA/2010/51.html
23 http://www.theregister.co.uk/2000/12/21/
    mobile_phone_user_found/
24 http://www.citmedialaw.org/haberman-v-rhoad
25 http://oh.findacase.com/research/wfrmDocViewer.aspx/xq/
    fac.20100128_0000165.NOH.htm/qx
26 http://www.abc.net.au/news/2011-07-21/
    hinch-sentenced-for-naming-sex-offenders/2804116
27 Burrows, J. & Cheer, U. (2005). Media Law in New Zealand.
    Fifth Edition. OUP, South Melbourne. p. 385.
28 http://epublications.bond.edu.au/hss_pubs/78/
29 http://www.telegraph.co.uk/technology/twitter/8540084/Judge-
    reports-Lord-Sugar-over-Twitter-post-on-expenses-trial.html
30 http://www.taylorwessing.com/download/news_110121.html
31 http://www.vgso.vic.gov.au/node/333
32 http://www.firstamendmentcenter.org/
    jurors-names-should-usually-be-released-rules-pa-high-court
33 http://juries.typepad.com/files/judge-sweeney.doc
34 http://twitter.com/#!/johnathan/status/1255697916

35 http://www.citmedialaw.org/threats/california-bar-v-wilson
36 http://cvillenews.com/2009/05/22/garrett-settles/
37 http://arstechnica.com/tech-policy/news/2009/06/texas-blogger-jailed-after-failing-to-turn-pc-over-to-judge.ars
38 http://www.blakedawson.com/Templates/Publications/x_article_content_page.aspx?id=54557

▶ **Chapter 4**

1 http://thelede.blogs.nytimes.com/2011/06/13/gay-girl-in-damascus-blogger-admits-to-writing-fiction-disguised-as-fact/
2 http://www.guardian.co.uk/commentisfree/2011/jun/13/open-door-anonymous-blogger
3 http://www.washingtonpost.com/blogs/blogpost/post/paula-brooks-editor-of-lez-get-real-also-a-man/2011/06/13/AGld2ZTH_blog.html
4 http://www.guardian.co.uk/world/2011/jun/26/gay-girl-damascus-accused-defending
5 http://www.msnbc.msn.com/id/43631406/ns/technology_and_science-security/t/hacked-fox-twitter-feed-reports-obamas-death/
6 http://www.dailytelegraph.com.au/news/lulzsec-hack-into-the-sun/story-e6freuy9-1226097306604
7 http://www.telegraph.co.uk/technology/twitter/8532683/Why-identifying-superinjunction-tweeters-may-not-be-easy.html
8 http://www.bailii.org/ew/cases/EWHC/QB/2008/1781.html
9 http://support.twitter.com/entries/18311-the-twitter-rules
10 http://www.themoscowtimes.com/news/article/fake-medvedev-twitter-account-is-closed/440364.html
11 https://www.facebook.com/terms.php
12 https://www.facebook.com/legal/copyright.php
13 http://www.star-telegram.com/2011/07/16/3225997/texas-has-tough-law-on-online.html
14 http://dallasmorningviewsblog.dallasnews.com/archives/2011/07/make-no-mistake.html
15 http://blogs.forbes.com/parmyolson/2011/05/30/thousands-like-fake-tupac-story-posted-by-hackers/
16 http://www.austlii.edu.au/cgi-bin/sinodisp/au/cases/cth/FCA/2011/74.html
17 http://en.rsf.org/kuwait-website-editor-freed-on-bail-after-22-08-2007,23347.html
18 http://news.bbc.co.uk/2/hi/americas/8099925.stm
19 http://www.guardian.co.uk/environment/georgemonbiot/2011/feb/23/need-to-protect-internet-from-astroturfing

20 http://www.rawstory.com/rs/wp-content/uploads/2011/03/
    personamanagementcontract.pdf
21 http://en.wikipedia.org/wiki/Anonymous_(group)#References
22 http://www.smh.com.au/technology/security/meet-the-hacktivist-
    who-tried-to-take-down-the-government-20110314-1btkt.html
23 http://blogs.forbes.com/
    luisakroll/2011/05/10/u-s-law-protects-anonymous-speech-not-
    billionaires/
24 http://www.sltrib.com/csp/cms/sites/sltrib/pages/printerfriendly.
    csp?id=51780456
25 http://www.forbes.com/sites/
    luisakroll/2011/05/10/u-s-law-protects-anonymous-speech-not-
    billionaires/
26 http://www.citmedialaw.org/threats/hester-v-home-henderson
27 http://homeinhenderson.com/2010/08/13/
    three-settle-with-hester-on-libel-suit/
28 http://caselaw.lp.findlaw.com/cgi-bin/getcase.
    pl?court=US&vol=362&invol=60
29 http://www.citmedialaw.org/sites/citmedialaw.org/files/2011-05-24-
    Denial%20of%20Protective%20Order.pdf
30 http://news.cnet.com/8301-31921_3-20042277-281.html
31 http://mobile.bloomberg.com/news/2011-11-10/wikileaks-backers-
    lose-appeal-of-order-giving-u-s-access-to-twitter-data
32 http://www.citmedialaw.org/threats/cohen-v-google-blogger
33 http://www.telegraph.co.uk/technology/twitter/8544350/Twitter-
    reveals-secrets-Details-of-British-users-handed-over-in-landmark-
    case-that-could-help-Ryan-Giggs.html
34 http://www.citmedialaw.org/directory/132
35 http://www.citmedialaw.org/threats/
    news-america-inc-v-google-inc-subpoena
36 http://www.bailii.org/uk/cases/UKHL/1973/6.html
37 http://www.gillhams.com/dictionary/556.cfm
38 http://www.bailii.org/ew/cases/EWHC/QB/2009/3148.html
39 http://www.dailymail.co.uk/news/article-1195399/Woman-branded-
    potentially-violent-council-complaining-damaged-flowerbed.html
40 http://www.bailii.org/ew/cases/EWHC/QB/2011/1164.html
41 http://www.canlii.org/en/on/onsc/doc/2011/2011onsc3023/2011
    onsc3023.html
42 http://ccla.org/2011/07/25/
    ontario-court-protects-political-speech-and-internet-anonymity/
43 http://www.lavanlegal.com.au/index.php/publications/
    publicationdetail/internet_defamation

44 http://www.ajr.org/Article.asp?id=4878
45 http://www.theaustralian.com.au/news/opinion/protect-confidential-sources/story-e6frg71x-1225922940209
46 http://www.theaustralian.com.au/business/media/controversial-political-blogger-unmasked-as-a-federal-public-servant/story-e6frg996-1225929679443
47 http://www.bailii.org/ew/cases/EWHC/QB/2009/1358.html
48 http://chronicle.com/blogs/onhiring/the-ethics-of-anonymity/29097?sid=at&utm_source=at&utm_medium=en
49 http://inforrm.wordpress.com/2011/06/11/hiding-behind-anonymity-%E2%80%93-lucy-middleton/

▶ **Chapter 5**

1 http://yalelawjournal.org/the-yale-law-journal/content-pages/the-two-western-cultures-of-privacy:-dignity-versus-liberty/
2 http://www.bailii.org/ew/cases/EWHC/QB/2011/1232.html
3 http://www.journalism.co.uk/news/journalist-could-face-jail-over-alleged-injunction-breach-on-twitter/s2/a544262/
4 http://www.bailii.org/ew/cases/EWHC/QB/2011/1308.html
5 http://www.inter-disciplinary.net/wp-content/uploads/2010/11/Rev1ever1111110.pdf
6 http://www.jjllplaw.com/The-Right-to-Privacy-Warren-Brandeis-Harvard-Law-Review-1890.html
7 http://www.splc.org/knowyourrights/legalresearch.asp?id=29
8 http://www.msnbc.msn.com/id/15221111/ns/technology_and_science-privacy_lost/t/la-difference-stark-eu-us-privacy-laws/
9 http://oecdprivacy.org/
10 http://www.economist.com/node/5389362
11 http://www.malaysianbar.org.my/human_rights/privacy_does_it_exist_in_malaysia_is_it_time_to_legislate_.html
12 http://www.caslon.com.au/privacyguide6.htm
13 http://www.tbplaw.com/data/Phot_Priv.pdf
14 http://www.lawlink.nsw.gov.au/lawlink/lrc/ll_lrc.nsf/pages/LRC_cp01chp5
15 http://www.newyorker.com/online/blogs/newsdesk/2011/05/dsk-french-lives-french-law.html
16 http://www.legislation.gov.uk/ukpga/1998/42/contents
17 http://www.bailii.org/ew/cases/EWCA/Civ/2005/595.html
18 http://www.bailii.org/uk/cases/UKHL/2004/22.html
19 http://www.bailii.org/eu/cases/ECHR/2004/294.html
20 http://www.bailii.org/ew/cases/EWCA/Civ/2006/1776.html

21 http://www.guardian.co.uk/media/2009/jul/13/
phone-hacking-timeline

22 http://www.telegraph.co.uk/news/uknews/theroyalfamily/2984685/
Princess-Diana-photographer-fined-for-invasion-of-privacy.html

23 http://www.telegraph.co.uk/news/1958074/Liz-Hurley-and-Hugh-
Grant-get-58000-damages-over-photographs.html

24 http://www.bailii.org/ew/cases/EWHC/QB/2008/1777.html

25 http://www.bailii.org/ew/cases/EWCA/Civ/2008/446.html

26 http://www.smh.com.au/technology/technology-news/uk-twitter-
users-banned-from-identifying-braindamaged-woman-20110516-
1eow5.html

27 http://www.guardian.co.uk/law/2011/may/20/
superinjunction-modern-technology-lord-judge

28 http://www.nzlii.org/cgi-bin/sinodisp/nz/cases/NZCA/2004/34.html

29 http://www.alrc.gov.au/publications/report-108

30 http://www.austlii.edu.au/au/cases/cth/high_ct/2001/63.html

31 http://ec.europa.eu/justice/policies/privacy/index_en.htm

32 http://www.sfgate.com/cgi-bin/article.cgi?f=/c/a/2005/03/24/
BAGFIBU2AT1.DTL

33 http://www.blogherald.com/2005/03/18/
kaiser-permanente-sues-blogger-over-patient-information/

34 http://www.myfox8.com/news/wghp-baptist-receives-letter-from-
attorney-generals-office-after-medical-record-theft-
20110603,0,4869603.story

35 http://www.cbc.ca/news/technology/story/2011/05/02/technology-
sony-playstation-data-breach.html

36 http://millerthomson.com/en/blog/ontario-insurance-litigation-blog/
sony-insurer-challenges-cyber-liability-claim

37 http://media2.myfoxdfw.com/PDF/facebook-suit.pdf

38 http://www.wired.com/threatlevel/2010/03/facebook-beacon-2/

39 http://www.supremecourt.gov/opinions/10pdf/09-1279.pdf

40 http://www.theage.com.au/opinion/society-and-culture/personal-
details-up-for-grabs-20110530-1fcp4.html

41 http://newsandinsight.thomsonreuters.com/Legal/News/2011/07_-_
July/A_new_law-enforcement_tool__Facebook_searches/

42 https://lacasacorp2010.appspot.com/www.eff.org/wp/
know-your-rights

43 http://www.eff.org/press/archives/2011/06/27

44 http://english.donga.com/srv/service.php3?biid=2011052706558

45 http://www.pewinternet.org/Media-Mentions/2011/Online-photos.aspx

46 http://www.abc.net.au/unleashed/2719142.html

47 http://arstechnica.com/tech-policy/news/2011/06/tenn-law-bans-posting-images-that-cause-emotional-distress.ars

48 http://www.bailii.org/ew/cases/EWHC/QB/2008/1781.html

49 http://www.leagle.com/xmlResult.aspx?xmldoc=In+TXCO+20080813428.xml&docbase=CSLWAR3-2007-CURR

50 http://www.redding.com/news/2008/feb/21/court-ends-dispute-over-blog/

51 http://mlrcblogsuits.blogspot.com/2009/04/duer-v.html

52 http://www.canlii.org/en/ns/nsca/doc/2011/2011nsca26/2011nsca26.html

▶ **Chapter 6**

1 http://or.findacase.com/research/wfrmDocViewer.aspx/xq/fac.19850306_0042709.OR.htm/qx

2 http://www.floridabar.org/DIVCOM/PI/RHandbook01.nsf/1119bd3 8ae090a748525676f0053b606/dfc00ac22467b7f5852569cb004cb c2a#C.%20Publication%20of%20Private%20Facts.

3 http://www.citmedialaw.org/legal-guide/publication-private-facts

4 http://www.law.upenn.edu/bll/archives/ulc/fnact99/1980s/utsa85.htm

5 http://gilc.org/privacy/survey/

6 http://www.libelandprivacy.com/areasofpractice_breachconfidence.html

7 http://www.bailii.org/ew/cases/EWHC/Ch/2010/2424.html

8 http://www.austlii.edu.au/au/cases/cth/high_ct/2001/63.html

9 http://www.citmedialaw.org/legal-guide/publication-private-facts

10 http://www.austlii.edu.au/au/cases/vic/VSC/2006/308.html

11 http://www.austlii.edu.au/au/legis/nsw/consol_act/ea199580/s126b.html

12 http://www.canlii.org/en/ca/scc/doc/2010/2010scc16/2010scc16.html

13 http://www.rcfp.org/reporters-privilege

14 http://www.legislation.gov.uk/ukpga/1981/49

15 http://www.legislation.govt.nz/act/public/2006/0069/latest/DLM393681.html?search=ts_act_citizenship_resel

16 http://en.rsf.org/france-court-cites-need-to-protect-11-05-2011,40269.html

17 http://en.rsf.org/ukraine-police-search-young-blogger-s-home-14-01-2011,39308.html

18 http://www.rcfp.org/newsitems/index.php?i=4701

19 http://online.wsj.com/article/SB10001424052748703296604576005 881472881282.html

20 http://www.thenewsmanual.net/Resources/medialaw_in_
australia_03.html
21 http://www.cpj.org/2010/07/ghana-police-criminally-prosecute-
journalist-over.php
22 http://cpj.org/2005/08/ethiopian-journalist-sent-to-jail-for-not-
identify.php
23 http://www.cpj.org/2009/08/after-al-qaeda-report-kenyan-police-
harass-star.php
24 http://www.crikey.com.au/2011/03/04/
journo-shield-law-covers-bloggers-independent-media/
25 http://www.citmedialaw.org/threats/
doty-v-molnar-subpoena-billings-gazette
26 http://www.reuters.com/article/2011/06/07/
us-newjersey-shield-idUSTRE7565Q520110607
27 http://latimesblogs.latimes.com/technology/2011/08/gizmodo-not-
motivated-by-financial-greed-in-iphone-case-da-says.html
28 http://www.citmedialaw.org/threats/
tsa-v-chris-elliott-and-steve-frischling
29 http://www.ignet.gov/randp/f01c10.pdf
30 http://www.bailii.org/ew/cases/EWHC/QB/2009/1358.html
31 http://www.austlii.edu.au/au/legis/nsw/consol_act/pida1994313/
s19.html
32 http://www.cio.co.uk/news/3211197/
mod-staff-leak-military-secrets-on-facebook-and-twitter/
33 http://www.nytimes.com/2011/06/08/us/08pentagon.
html?_r=1&pagewanted=1
34 http://www.nytimes.com/books/97/04/13/reviews/papers-final.html
35 http://www.washingtonpost.com/wp-dyn/content/
article/2006/01/14/AR2006011401165.html
36 http://www.bbc.co.uk/news/technology-12492933

▶ Chapter 7

1 http://www.washingtonpost.com/wp-dyn/content/
article/2006/02/17/AR2006021702499.html
2 http://edition.cnn.com/2002/WORLD/africa/11/22/nigeria.miss.
world/index.html
3 http://www.telegraph.co.uk/news/worldnews/northamerica/
canada/3498766/Facebook-Kick-a-Ginger-campaign-prompts-
attacks-on-redheads.html
4 http://www.austlii.edu.au/au/cases/qld/QCA/2011/132.html
5 http://pacer.ca4.uscourts.gov/opinion.pdf/101098.P.pdf

6   http://genocidepreventionnow.org/Portals/0/docs/Bazyler-GPN-
    Original.pdf
7   http://www.wiesenthal.com/site/apps/nlnet/content2.aspx?c=lsKWL
    bPJLnF&b=4441467&ct=9141065
8   http://www.hatedirectory.com/hatedir.pdf
9   http://www.citmedialaw.org/sites/citmedialaw.org/files/2010-06-28-
    Opinion%20reversing%20district%20court's%20dismissal.pdf
10 http://www.richardwarman.ca/?page_id=2
11 http://www.chrt-tcdp.gc.ca/search/files/t869_11903de.pdf
12 http://www.chrc-ccdp.ca/proactive_initiatives/hoi_hsi/qa_qr/
    page1-eng.aspx
13 http://chrt-tcdp.gc.ca/aspinc/search/vhtml-eng.
    asp?doid=981&lg=_e&isruling=0
14 http://www.abc.net.au/pm/stories/s65901.htm
15 http://law.justia.com/cases/federal/appellate-courts/
    F3/433/1199/546158/
16 http://news.cnet.com/8301-17852_3-10237855-71.html
17 http://www.bbc.co.uk/news/uk-scotland-tayside-central-14392082
18 http://www.bbc.co.uk/news/uk-scotland-tayside-central-14380910
19 http://www.telegraph.co.uk/news/worldnews/europe/
    netherlands/8593559/Geert-Wilders-acquitted-on-hate-speech-
    charges.html
20 http://www.iheu.org/
    iheu-calls-abolition-africa%E2%80%99s-blasphemy-laws
21 http://www.lawlink.nsw.gov.au/lrc.nsf/pages/DP24CHP3
22 http://www.brentonpriestley.com/writing/blasphemy.htm
23 http://www.cancrime.com/2011/07/24/
    convict-taunts-attackers-in-profane-slur-in-fb-video/
24 http://www.ca9.uscourts.gov/datastore/opinions/2011/07/19/09-
    50529.pdf
25 http://www.hreoc.gov.au/racial_discrimination/cyberracism/
    vilification.html
26 http://www.msnbc.msn.com/id/43135427/ns/us_news-crime_and_
    courts/t/not-guilty-plea-entered-teen-rutgers-webcam-case/#.
    TlG6rnPl2MJ
27 http://www.people.com/people/article/0,,1219142,00.html
28 http://www.thesun.co.uk/sol/homepage/showbiz/bizarre/3076084/
    Joe-McElderry-admits-that-he-is-gay.html
29 http://www.lawlink.nsw.gov.au/adtjudgments/2004nswadt.nsf/731b7
    18ec02a5793ca25684e00413824/aa30febf688a7946ca256f500007
    bc0f?OpenDocument

30 http://www.news.com.au/top-stories/pillow-biter-win-for-laws/
    story-e6frfkp9-1111113081686
31 http://www.dailymail.co.uk/sciencetech/article-1322916/Facebook-
    accidentally-outing-gay-users-advertisers.html

▶ **Chapter 8**

1   http://jezebel.com/5809063/forever-21-sues-fashion-blogger
2   http://wtforever21.wordpress.com/2011/06/28/873/
3   http://www.huffingtonpost.com/rachel-kane/forever-21-columbus-
    day_b_1000788.html
4   http://www.wipo.int/directory/en/urls.jsp
5   http://www.wipo.int/freepublications/en/intproperty/909/wipo_
    pub_909.html
6   http://creativecommons.org/
7   http://www.wipo.int/freepublications/en/intproperty/909/wipo_
    pub_909.html
8   http://www.bjp-online.com/british-journal-of-photography/
    news/2101942/bbc-caught-twitter-copyright-row
9   http://www.citmedialaw.org/threats/
    zomba-recording-llc-v-lavandeira
10 http://canyoucopyrightatweet.com/
11 http://www.wipo.int/freepublications/en/intproperty/909/wipo_
    pub_909.html
12 http://www.wired.com/threatlevel/2011/09/
    righthaven-nearing-bankruptcy/
13 http://www.wipo.int/amc/en/domains/casesx/all.html
14 http://www.pbs.org/mediashift/2011/04/facebook-sometimes-slow-
    to-remove-offensive-content-fake-profiles104.html
15 http://www.inta.org/Media/Pages/TrademarkChecklist.aspx
16 http://blog.internetcases.com/about/library/
    facebook-inc-v-teachbook-com/
17 http://www.huffingtonpost.com/2010/07/26/fired-over-facebook-
    posts_n_659170.html#s115707&title=Swiss_Woman_Caught
18 http://www.ftc.gov/opa/2009/10/endortest.shtm
19 http://www.insidecounsel.com/2011/07/12/
    ip-ftc-advertising-enforcement-on-social-media

▶ **Chapter 9**

1   http://singaporedissident.blogspot.com/2008_11_01_archive.html
2   http://www.un.org/en/documents/udhr/index.shtml
3   http://www.firstamendmentcenter.org/sofa

4 http://www.sfgate.com/cgi-bin/article.cgi?f=/c/a/2007/04/03/
BAGLRP0PAP4.DTL
5 http://articles.timesofindia.indiatimes.com/2009-05-10/
mumbai/28172842_1_vikram-buddhi-iranian-american-journalist-
online-threat
6 http://www.eff.org/files/filenode/dorders_twitter/MemOpinion.pdf
7 http://www.echr.coe.int/NR/rdonlyres/CA9986C0-BF79-4E3D-
9E36-DCCF1B622B62/0/FICHES_New_technologies_EN.pdf
8 http://en.rsf.org/press-freedom-index-2010,1034.html
9 http://www.guardian.co.uk/media/2011/may/10/
echr-max-mosley-conclusion
10 http://www.humanrightsinitiative.org/publications/chogm/
chogm_2003/country chart.pdf
11 http://www.dfat.gov.au/facts/democratic_rights_freedoms.html
12 http://www.nzlii.org/nz/cases/NZSC/2011/45.html
13 http://www.yalelawtech.org/censorship/
censorship-in-the-digital-age/
14 http://thailand-business-news.com/asean/
30373-burma-grants-amnesty-but-steps-up-internet-surveillance
15 http://www.indexoncensorship.org/2011/08/
china-outspoken-blogger-released-after-six-months-in-detention/
16 http://www.telegraph.co.uk/technology/news/8679658/China-chief-
suspect-in-major-cyber-attack.html
17 http://www.smh.com.au/technology/technology-news/australia-to-
defend-itself-in-cyber-war-20110602-1fizx.html
18 http://www.bangkokpost.com/lite/topstories/252639/
us-disappointed-by-lese-majeste-charge
19 http://news.bbc.co.uk/2/hi/6498297.stm
20 http://www.guardian.co.uk/uk/2010/nov/11/
twitter-joke-trial-appeal-verdict
21 http://www.news.com.au/technology/hacker-croll-says-obama-
britney-twitter-hacks-were-a-warning/
story-e6frfro0-1225845828996
22 http://www.thenewsmanual.net/Resources/medialaw_in_
australia_06.html
23 http://www.privacy.org.au/Resources/APH-Lib-terrorism-
071008.htm
24 http://frwebgate.access.gpo.gov/cgi-bin/getdoc.cgi?dbname=107_
cong_public_laws&docid=f:publ056.107.pdf
25 http://ottawa.ctv.ca/servlet/an/local/CTVNews/20110630/OTT_
Khawaja_110630/20110630/?hub=OttawaHome

26 http://www.theaustralian.com.au/news/nation/terror-accused-belal-khazaal-granted-bail-ahead-of-trial/story-e6frg6nf-1226089789442
27 http://www.google.com/transparencyreport/governmentrequests/
28 http://www.bbc.co.uk/news/technology-10692501
29 http://news.smh.com.au/breaking-news-technology/2-mexicans-deny-terrorism-face-30-years-for-tweet-20110905-1jssa.html
30 http://news.smh.com.au/breaking-news-technology/2-mexicans-deny-terrorism-face-30-years-for-tweet-20110905-1jssa.html
31 http://www.guardian.co.uk/world/2011/sep/04/twitter-terrorists-face-30-years

INDEX

A Gay Girl In Damascus blog
    63–4
ABC, Behrendt case 9
absence of malice defence 15–16
absolute privilege 33
account of profits claims 115
Adelaide Institute 135
Adelman, Lynn 132–3
admissibility of evidence 28–9
Afghanistan 138
Africa 42, 138, 174, *see also*
    names of African states
Algeria 138
Al-Sayegh, Bashar 69–70, 176
amends, offer of 35
American Civil Liberties Union
    75, 81
American Convention on Human
    Rights 90–1, 131
American Declaration of the
    Rights and Duties of Man
    90, 131
American Journalism Review 82
American National Socialist
    Workers Party 132
Amnesty International 182–3
Anderson, Diane 55

anonymity 63–85
'Anonymous' hacker group 72
Anti-Discrimination Act (NSW)
    142
anti-Islamic sites 137
anti-terrorism, *see* terrorism laws
apologies 35
Apple 119
appropriation 90
Arbitration and Mediation Center
    161
Argentina 110
Arraf, Amina 63–4
Asia, defamation law in 41
Asian Human Rights Commission
    174
Assange, Julian 46, 49, 75–6, *see*
    also WikiLeaks case
Associated Press 182
astroturfing 71
attorney–client privilege 116
attribution of the creator 154
audio streaming, fair use and 153
Australasian Legal Information
    Institute 187
Australia
    Constitution of 173

Defamation Acts 2005–6 38
duty to disclose in 81
Federal Court 69, 136
free expression in 173
hate speech laws 140, 142
High Court rulings 4–5
journalists jailed in 118
Lenah Game Meats case 111
new shield laws 119
privacy rights and protections
    96
Rindos v Hardwick 37
take-down notices in 52
terrorism laws 179
Australian, The (newspaper) 82–3
Australian Broadcasting
    Commission, Behrendt case
    9
Australian Capital Territory,
    service of writs in 61–2
Australian Football League
    115–16
Australian Law Reform
    Commission 96
Austria 185
authors' rights 150
Ayers, Bob 132

Bacon, Louis 73
Bagdasarian, Walter 139–40
Baker, Justice 95
Barber, Jeremiah xlv
Barron's 4
Bass, Lance 141
Baumgartner, Elsebeth 55
BBC 6, 154
Behrendt, Larissa 9
Belarus 172, 176
Belgium 40
Bennett, Mark 47
Berkman Center for Internet and
    Society 186
Berne Convention 149, 151

*Best Served Cold – Studies in
    Revenge* 88
Bettencourt, Liliane 118
bigotry 125–44
Bill of Rights (New Zealand) 173
Billings Gazette 119
Bilozerska, Olena 118
Birmingham police force (UK),
    Twitter use 47
Black, Justice 74
blasphemy laws 138–9
'blawgers' 189
Blevins, Nate 175
Blishen, Justice 80
Blockbuster 98
Blogetery site 181
Blogger.com, *see* Google
blogging
    as evidence 60–1
    cybersquatting rules 161
    hate sites 131–4
    intellectual property and
        148–9
    job loss over 163
    legal restrictions on 169
    need to check in 17
    online comments 142
    satirical blogs 103–4
    shield laws and 119–20
    WordPress 17, 73, 161
Boland, Boyd N. 74–5
Bombay High Court 7
Boudoir Queen label 19
Brady, Duane 42
Brand, Dave 137
Brandeis, Louis D. 89
Brazil 110
breach of confidence 109–12,
    114–15
breach of contract 11
Britain, *see* United Kingdom
British and Irish Legal
    Information Institute 187

British Broadcasting Corporation 6, 154
British Commonwealth, *see* Commonwealth of Nations
Brodkorb, Michael 34
Brooks, Paula 64
Brown, Evan 190
Brown, Judge 32
Brunei 176
Buck, James Karl 47
Buddhi, Vikram S. 171
Bulgaria 110
bullying, online 68, 103–5
burden of proof, defamation cases 30
Burma 174–5
Burst.net 181
Bush, George W. 171

California Department of Managed Health Care 97–8
Campbell, Naomi 93, 108
Canada
anonymity request refused 48
confidentiality in 116–17
court rules on hyperlinks 10
cyberbullying protections 105
defamation law 37
duty to disclose in 80–1
Facebook case 139
human rights campaigns 134–5
Supreme Court rulings 10, 38
terrorism laws 180
Canadian Charter of Rights and Freedoms 134
Canadian Civil Liberties Union 81
Canadian Human Rights Act 135
Canadian Human Rights Tribunal 134–5
Canadian Legal Information Institute 187

Caroline of Monaco case 94
Caslon Analytics 91–2
Castan, Melissa 192
Castro, Antonio 70
celebrities
attempts to shield 88
confidentiality protections 108
copyright issues 159–60
public interest and 34
suits brought by 93–5
trial by media 49–50
UK law and 172–3
Celtics football team 137
censorship regimes 28, 36, 166–83, *see also* free expression rights
Center for Democracy and Technology 81–2
Centre for Socio-Legal Studies 40
Chambers, Paul 178
Charles, Prince of Wales 94
Chen, Jason 119
China 41, 91, 175
Chronicle (Orange County, NY) 77–8
Chronicle of Higher Education 83
Citizen Media Law Project 54, 77–8, 109, 114–15, 186
Civil Liberties Union 75, 81
civil suits vs criminal offences 10–11
Clancco: Art and Law site 190
Clark High School, Texas 104
Clementi, Tyler 121, 141
Clift, Jane 79–80
Cluck, Robert 68
Cohen, Liskula 76
Collins, Ben 111
Colorado District Court 74
Columbia Journalism Review 162
commercial litigation 147

Committee to Protect Journalists 118–19, 184
common law heritage 173
Commonwealth of Nations, *see also* names of Commonwealth states
confidentiality protections 110–13
defamation law 37–8
defences to breach of confidence 114
duty to disclose in 80–2
free expression in 173–4
privacy rights and protections 96
Communications Decency Act (US) 23, 69, 79
compensation claims 115
confidence, breach of 109–12, 114–15
confidential sources, *see also* shield laws
leaks from 107
protecting 28, 32–3
shielding 116–19
confidentiality 107–24
conflict of laws 3
conspiracy theories 56
constitutional protections to free expression 28, *see also* First Amendment to the US Constitution
Contemporary Business News 7
contempt in the face of the court 53–4
contempt of court 52–61
Contempt of Court Act (UK) 117
contract, breach of 11
Convention Establishing the World Intellectual Property Organisation 148
Cooley, Thomas 89
Cooper, Elisa 97–8

copyright issues 14, 149–60
corporations, can sue for defamation 10
court orders, defiance of 54–6, *see also* injunctions
court reporting 25–6, 45–62
Cousteix, François 178–9
Cowdroy, Dennis 47
creations of the mind 148–9
Creative Commons organisation 152
crimen injuria 42
criminal offences 10–11, 21, 40
Cu Huy Ha Vu xiv–xv
Cullen, Trevor 6
cvillenews.com blog 60
cyberbullying protections 103–5
CyberSLAPP.org 81
cybersquatting 160–1
cyberstalking 103–5

Daily Mail 79
Daimler case 26
damages in defamation cases 35–6
Dangdai Shang Bao 7
Data Protection Directive 97
data protection laws 97–9
Datamotion Asia Pacific Ltd 81
dead, ability of to sue 21–2
deceptive conduct 63–85, 163
declarations of falsehood 35–6
deep links 157
defamation 19–43
hospital sues for ix
public interest defence 14
regional variations in 36–42
Defamation Act (Australia) 38
defences
to breach of confidence 114–15
to defamation 27–8
DeGeneres, Ellen 141

delict, law of 92
Deluca, Michael 77
Denmark 57, 125–6, 176
Denver Post xiii–xiv
Diana, Princess of Wales 93–4
DiBiase, Tad xiii–xiv
digital archiving, legal status of
    13
digital fingerprints 99–103
Directory of Intellectual Property
    Offices 149
disclosure of iniquity defence
    120
Dolan, Christopher 164
domain names 160–1
Dominguez, Luis 70
Doolittle-Norby, Beth 104
Douglas, Michael 93, 108
Dow Jones v Gutnick (Australia)
    4–5
Draker, Anna 104
Duer, Melissa 104–5
Dumas, Alexandre 86–7
duties, rights and xvi–xvii

Eady, Justice 87, 121
EFF, *see* Electronic Frontier
    Foundation
Egypt 47, 138, 176
Electronic Frontier Foundation
    as member of CyberSLAPP.org
        82
    contact details 185
    Denver Post case xiii–xiv
    Know Your Rights website
        100–1
    Legal Guide for Bloggers 39
    WikiLeaks case 75
*Electronic Information and
    Transaction Law Act*
    (Indonesia) 42
Electronic Privacy Information
    Center 82

Elliott, Chris 120
Ellsberg, Daniel 121–2
enemies of the state 168–9
England, *see* United Kingdom
Entertainment Law podcast 190
Erasing David (documentary) 100
Erdodi, Joshua 139
Estonia 110
Ethiopia 119
Europe, *see also* names of
        European states
    blasphemy laws 139
    confidentiality protections 110
    data protection laws 97
    defamation law 40–1
    freedom of expression in
        171–2
    privacy rights and protections
        92
    sub judice contempt in 57
European Convention on Human
        Rights
    Article 6 48
    Article 8 110, 173
    Article 10 171–2
    incorporated into UK law 93,
        172
    on rights 131
    privacy rights and protections
        90, 92
    UK and 37
European Court of Human Rights
        91, 94, 171–2
Evidence Act (NSW) 116
Evidence Act (NZ) 117
exposure of iniquity 114
extradition 6–7

Facebook
    anonymity request refused 48
    case against Teachbook 162–3
    confidentiality of 111
    copyright infringement on 17

cybersquatting rules 161
Daimler case 26
defamation cases xiv, 22–4
'Facebook Beacon' cases 98–9
fake profiles 161–2
Fraill case 45
French cases 40–1
'friending' the accused 59
Holocaust denial sites 136
privacy breaches on 142
racial hatred on 139
requests to search 100
responsibility for user
    comments on 69
South African cases 42
spoof accounts 67–8, 103
Statement of Rights 67, 161
Tupac Shakur case 68
facial recognition technology 102
*Faconnable USA Corporation v
    John Does 1–10* (US) 74–5
fair comment 30–1
fair dealing 152–4
fair use defences 14, 152–4
fairness requirements 33
Fakhoury, Hanni 101
false light 90
Fayed, Dodi 94
Federal Trade Commission (US)
    163
Feingold, Jason 73–4
Finland 172
Firsht, Mathew 67
First Amendment Center 55,
    185, 191
First Amendment to the US
    Constitution 14–15
defamation law and 38–9
defences to breach of
    confidence 114–15
free expression under 131,
    170–1

limited to US cases 167–8
on publication of proceedings
    53
privacy rights and protections
    89–90
protects satirical blogs 104
Flickr, Chang case 1–2
Forever 21 45–7
Forgotten Ohio website 104–5
forwarding posts 9–10
Fox News Twitter accounts 64
Fraill, Joanne 45
France
    confidentiality protections 110
    defamation cases 40–1
    press laws 118
    privacy rights and protections
        89, 92
    Yahoo! Holdings case 136
France Dimanche 94
Franklin, Raymond A. 131
Fraser, Jason 94
free expression rights 28, 169
free use 152–4
Freedom House 178
freedom of information requests
    99
Freedominion board 80
freedomsite.org 135
FreeSpeech Daily 192
Frischling, Steve 120
Fry, Stephen 12–13

gag orders, *see* injunctions
GalaxyFacts 77
Gault, Justice 96
Gay Girl in Damascus blog 63–4
Gay News 138–9
Gazette of Law and Journalism 188
geolocation capabilities 101–2,
    122
George, Matthew 72

Germany
    blasphemy laws 139
    court reporting in 47
    Holocaust denial laws 131,
        135–6
    privacy rights and protections
        92
Getaped.com Inc v Cangemi (US)
    4–5
Ghana 119
Giffords, Gabrielle 140
Gillhams 72, 78
Gizmodo site 119
Glennon, Michael 55
Global Internet Liberty Campaign
    110
Goodman, Clive 94
Google
    Gremach case 7
    ordered to identify blogger 76
    requests for injunction on 78
    Transparency Reports 181
Gopnik, Adam 92
Gordon, Joe 176
governments
    confidentiality tests 113
    enemies of the state 168–9
    information leaked 122
Graber, Bill 64
Grant, Hugh 94
Grant, Peter 38
Great Firewall of China 175
Greece 176, 192
Green, David Allen 189
Greenpeace 179
Gremach company 7
Grog's Gamut blog 82–3
Guardian newspaper 64, 71
Gutnick, Joseph 4, 25

'Hacker Croll' 178–9
hacking 65, 88, 102
Hadjis, Athanasios 135

Hale, Matthew 132–3
Hampson, Bradley 129
harassment, *see* bullying online
Harrington, Lyndal 60–1
Harris, Cathryn 98
Harvard Law Review 89
Hate Directory 131
hate speech 131–4
Hellerstein, Alvin 4–5
Hello! magazine 93, 108
Henderson, Andrew 104–5
Hezbollah 75
High Commissioner for Human
        Rights 170
Hilton, Perez 141, 154
Hinch, Derryn 55
Hitler, Adolf 136
Hoffmann, Mark P. 133
Holocaust denial laws 131, 135–6
Home In Henderson blog 73–4
homosexuality, hate speech laws
        140–2
honest opinion 30–1
Hong Kong 7
Horton, Richard 120–1
Hosking, Mike and Marie 96
hospital sues for defamation ix
hosts, *see* ISPs
HotCopper 81
Ho-Wee Wong, Justin 1–2
Howling Pig 21
Huffington Post 147, 163
Human Rights Act (Canada) 135
Human Rights Act (UK) 93, 108,
        172
Human Rights and Equal
        Opportunity Commission
        (Australia) 136
Hurley, Liz 94
hyperlinking
    Canadian court rules on 10
    copyright issues 156–7
    defamation and 24

ICANN 160
Iceland 172
identification 63–85
    identity theft legislation 98
    of persons referred to 25–6
    through Internet activity 100
impersonation 67–8
imputation, defamatory 29
independence, price of 8
India 54, 173
Indonesia 42
in-house counsel 8
injunctions 51–2
    breach of confidence cases 115
    defamation cases 35–6
    in the UK 95
    super injunctions 51, 95
injurious falsehood 21
innuendo 26
intellectual property
    blogging and 148–9
    copyright issues 14, 149, 151
    trademark law 162–3
Intellectual Property Organisation
    148–9
International Center For
    Journalists 185
International Covenant on Civil
    and Political Rights
    Article 19 169–70
    on incitement to hatred 131
    privacy rights and protections
        90–1
International Forum for
    Responsible Media 186
International Humanist and
    Ethical Union 138
International Media Lawyers
    Association 187
International Monetary Fund 92
International Press Institute 185
International Trademark
    Association 162

Internet
    identity traces left on 100
    immediacy of 12–13
Internet Corporation for Assigned
    Names and Numbers 160
Internet service providers, *see*
    ISPs
intrusion 90
IP Law Updates 190
Iran 126, 138, 174
Ireland 178–9, 189
Islamic states 64, 126–7, 137–8
ISPs
    best practice for 81
    liability for defamation 23
    liability of 69, 134
    pressure on 7
    responsibility of 8
Italy, defamation cases 40

Jackson, Michael 49
Jackson, Peter 34
jail terms 20–1, 69–70, 118–19
Japan 41, 174
Jaquith, Waldo 60
Jenkins, Rob 83
Jericho, Greg 82–3
Jones, Jeremy 136
Journalism Review 82, 162
journalists 82, 118–19
Judge, Lord 95
Judge Judy 49
Julian Assange 171
jurisdiction issues 5–7
jurors, disclosure about 58–9
just cause or excuse 114
Justia.com 188
justified disclosure 114
Jyllands-Posten 125

Kaiser Permanente Health Group
    97
Kakao Talk 101

Kane, Rachel 145–7
Kazakhstan 176
Kenya 119
Khawaja, Momin 180
Khazaal, Belal Saadalah 180
Khomeini, Ayatollah Ruhollah 126
Kidman, Nicole 34
Kimball, Dale 73
Know Your Rights website 100–1
Koch Industries 73
Konstantakopoulos, Theodore
    192
Kowalski, Kara 129–30
Kuwait 69–70, 176
Kyu Yu Houm 191

Lam-MacLeod, Kay 191
Lane, Sean 98–9
Las Vegas Review-Journal xiv
Latin America, defamation law
    42
Latvia 110
Laws, John 142
Le Monde 118
Le Nguyen Huong Tra 42
Leagle, Inc. 188
leaks, see also WikiLeaks case
    from confidential sources 107
    from governments 122
Lecic, Jelena 64
legacy media, in-house counsel 8
Legal Guide for Bloggers 39
Legalis.net 188
Lemire, Marc 134–5
Lenah Game Meats case
    (Australia) 96, 111–12
Leong, James 167
Lerner, Slava 77
lese-majesty 176
LexisNexis 192–3
Lez Get Real website 64
liability 9, 42–3
libel, see also defamation

criminal penalties 40
defined 20
liability for 42–3
requirements for case 9
seditious libel 20
licensing copyright 155
linking, see hyperlinking
Lochrie, Christy 104
Love, Courtney 19–20, 26
LulzSec group 65, 68

MacMaster, Tom 63–4
Mail on Sunday newspaper 94
Malaysia 41, 91
Maldives 94, 176
malice 15–16, 31, see also
    defamation
Manning, Bradley 122
Maremont, Jill xiii
Markus, David 51–2
McConchie Law Corporation
    110–11
McElderry, Joe 141
McVicker, William 77
Media Guardian 191
medical data, protection for
    97–8, 110
medium, legal issues and 16–17
Medvedev, Dmitry 67
Meeja Law website 191
Mein Kampf 136
Menken, Adah Isaacs 86–7
Mexico, terrorism laws in 181–2
Middle East 122, 174
Middleton, Lucy 84
Miller, Judith 118
Miller Thomson 98
Milum, David 22–3
Mink, Thomas 21
Miranda warning 60
Mirror newspaper 93, 108
misleading and deceptive conduct
    63–85, 163

misrepresentation 165
mobile phones, use in court 54, 59
Mohammed cartoons case 125–6
Moir, Ronald 81
Mondoweiss website 64
Montenegro 172
Moore, Craig 190
moral rights 67, 158
Morocco 176
Morozov, Evgeny 190
Morris v Johnson (Canada) 80–1
Morse, Valerie 173–4
Mosley, Max 94, 172–3
Mostrous, Alexi 46
Mulcaire, Glenn 94
Mulyasari, Prita 42
Murdoch, Rupert 65
Muslim states 64, 126–7, 138
MySpace 104, 129

Nair, Gopalan 166–7
National Post newspaper 117
Nay Phone Latt 175
Nayar, Arun 94
negligence ix, 104
Neo-Nazi groups 132–3, 136
Netherlands 137, 172, 176
New England First Amendment
    Center 191
New Sunday Herald 87
New York Post 78
New York Supreme Court 76
New York Times 38, 51, 118, 122
New York Times v Sullivan (US)
    38–9
New Zealand
    Bill of Rights 173–4
    blasphemy laws 138
    Court of Appeal 96
    Evidence Act 117
    privacy rights and protections
    96

Supreme Court rulings 173
    terrorism laws 179
Newcastle Herald 59
News America 78
News International 64–5
News of the World 64–5, 88, 94,
    172–3
newspaper rule 61
Nicolaides, Harry 176
Niemeyer, Judge 129–30
Nigeria 126, 138
Night Jack blog 83, 120–1
No Phat Pink Chicks blog 104
*Nolo's Plain-English Law
    Dictionary* 52
North Carolina Superior Court
    73
North Korea 174
Norway 126, 172
*Norwich Pharmacal v
    Commissioners of Customs
    and Excise* (UK) 72, 78–9

Obama, Barack
    denounces cyberbullying 141
    hate sites against 139–40
    Twitter account broken into
    179
obligation of confidence 112
O'Dell, Eoin 189
O'Donnell, Leanne 191
offer of amends 35
OK! magazine 108
online comments 142
online harassment laws 68
Ontario Superior Court 80
open comments forums 70
open justice 48–9
opinion 30–2, 125–44
Organisation for Economic
    Co-operation and
    Development (OECD) 91
Overthrow.com site 132–3

Pakistan 127, 138
Papua New Guinea 173
Parliament of Australia 188
passing off 159
passwords, choice of 101
PBS 68, 161
Peake, Junius 21
Pearson, Mark ix, 191
Pennsylvania Supreme Court 58
Pentagon Papers 121–2
People magazine 141
personal privacy, defining 99
personal vendettas 128–30
personality rights 159
Perugia Shock blog 52
Peter, Andrew 193
Pew Research Center 102
Pharmacal 72, 78–9
Phat and Pink blog 104
photographs 102–3, 153, 159
Pillay, Navi 138
plaintiffs, in US law 39
Plame, Valerie 118
PlayStation Network hacking 98
Poland 176
Portugal 42
Posetti, Julie xiv
preventative closure orders 52
Pribetic, Antonin I. 189
Price, Bess 9
Prince Charles of Wales 94
Prince William, Duke of
    Cambridge 94
Princess Caroline of Monaco 94
Princess Diana of Wales 93–4
prior restraint rules 36, 168–9
privacy rights and protections
    88–105
PrivacyInternational.org 91
PrivacyMemes 192
protected reporting 32–3
protection of sources 56, 66, 107,
    116–19

'Provisions on the Rules of Jihad'
    180
pseudonyms, use of 65–6, 72–8,
    83–4
Public Broadcasting Service (US)
    68, 161
Public Citizen 82
public disclosure of embarrassing
    facts 90
public figures, *see* celebrities
public interest
    as defence 34
    blogging in 13–15
    deception in 70–1
    protections for whistleblowers
        120
Public Interest Disclosures Act
    (NSW) 121
publication, defined 25
publishers, defined xv

quality of confidence 111
Queensland Police Force,
    Facebook pages 47
Queer Eye for the Straight Guy 142
quotation
    fair use and 153
    of defamatory remarks 29
    user-generated content 69–70

Racial Discrimination Act
    (Australia) 136
racial hatred 139–40
Radio Free Asia xv
Ran Yunfei 175
Ravi, Dharun 141
Record Searchlight 104
redheads, hate crimes against
    128
regional variations in defamation
    36–42
registration of copyright 152

religious sensibilities 126–7,
137–9
remedies for defamation 35–6,
104, 115
Reporters Committee for
Freedom of the Press 117,
186
Reporters Without Borders
condemns Nair judgement 166
contact details 185
on enemies of free speech
174–5
pressure on France to change
laws 118
World Press Freedom Index
172, 178
resources 184–95
responsible journalism in
Commonwealth law 37–8
Reuters 100
Reynolds case (UK) 38
Rhoad, Kristen 54
Riddle, Howard 46
ridicule 26–7
Rieder, Rem 82
Righthaven cases xiv, 157
rights, see also copyright issues
duties and xvi–xvii
infringements of 130–1
moral rights 158
privacy rights 88–105
right to be forgotten 100
right to confidentiality of
correspondence 110
right to publicity 159–60
Rindos v Hardwick (Australia) 37
Robertson, Geoffrey 4
Room 8 (political website) 51
Rooney, Ian 137
Rose, Flemming 126
Rowling, J.K. 94
royal family, insulting 175–6
Rozenberg, Joshua 190

Rushdie, Salman 36, 126
Russia 67, 172
Rutgers University 141
Ruzal, Scott 47
Rwanda 173

SASH MySpace page 129–30
satire 30–2, 103–4
Saudi Arabia 174
Saunders, Justice 57
scandalising the court 56
Scandinavia, see names of states
Scotland, see United Kingdom
security laws 166–83
sedition laws 179
seditious libel 20
self-regulation 161–2
serving of legal documents 61–2
sex crime victims 50
Shakur, Tupac 68
Sharia laws 127
Sharp, Justice 79–80
Shera, Rick 189
Shi Tao case 7
shield laws 56, 66, 107, 116–19
Silverman, Justin 191
Simon Wiesenthal Center 131
Simons, Margaret 48
Simorangkir, Dawn 19
Singapore, defamation law 41–2,
166–7
Singapore Dissident 166–7
Skanks in NYC blog 76
slander 20, see also defamation
SLAPP writs 24
Slough Borough Council 79
Smith, Anna Nicole, mother of
sues for defamation 61
social media, see blogging;
Facebook; MySpace;
Twitter; WordPress
Social Media Law website 192
Sony, data lost by 98

South Africa 38, 42, 120
South America 110, 174
South Korea, defamation law 41
South Park 128
South Tyneside Council case 5,
    23–4, 76–7
Southern District of Florida blog
    51–2
Spain 42, 176
Spears, Britney 154, 179
sponsorship, disclosing 163–4
spoof accounts 67–8
Springfield News-Leader 78
stop writs, *see* injunctions
Strategic Lawsuits Against Public
    Participation 24
Strauss-Kahn, Dominique 92
strict liability 28
sub judice contempt 56–8
Subordinate Courts 167
subpoenas against bloggers, etc
    60
Sudan 138
Suffolk Media Law 187, 191
Sugar, Lord Alan 57
Sullivan, Bob 90
summons, service of 61–2
Sun newspaper 65, 87, 141
super injunctions 51, 95
suppression orders, *see*
    injunctions
Sutherland, Kate 191
Sweden 40, 172
Sweeney, Dennis 59
Switzerland 110, 172, 176
Sydney Morning Herald 72
Syria 63, 175–6
Szymanski, David 55

take-down notices 52
Talley v California (US) 74
Tasmania 96
Taylor, Lord 57

Taylor Wessing 57
Teachbook case 162–3
Telegraph newspaper
    Fry case 12
    on redhead hate campaign 128
    Taylor case 57
    Twitter case 76
    Wilders case 137
terrorism laws 179–82
Thailand 175–6, 183
The Howling Pig 21
third parties, liability of 9
threats, legality of 11–12
Times newspaper 46, 51, 83, 121
Töben, Frederick 135–6
Top Gear 111
Toplitt, Sheldon 189
Toronto Star 38
tort, defamation as 20
Townsend, Judith 191
'Toxic Writer' blog 7
trade libel 21
trademark law 162–3
transferring copyright 154–5
Transparency Reports 181
Transportation Security
    Administration directive
    (US) 120
travelling, need for care when
    177–8
treason laws 179
'trial by media' 49, 56
Trib Total Media 77
TripAdvisor 31
Trummel, Paul 54
truth as a defence to defamation
    28–30
Turkey 7, 59
Turkmenistan 175
Twelve Angry Men 58
Twitter
    attribution issues 154
    copyright issues 16–17, 154

court reporting via 46–8
footballer case xviii, 51
for live reporting xiv
Fox News accounts 64
Fry case 12–13
hacked accounts 179
impersonation on 162
Malaysian cases 41
ordered to release account
    information 75–6
responsibility for user
    comments on 69
retweeting on 9–10
South Tyneside Council case
    5, 23–4, 76–7
Twitter Rules 67
US government obliges to
    disclose information 171
typosquatting 161

UK Independence Party 23
Ukraine 118
UN, *see* United Nations
'Understanding Copyright and
    Related Rights' 150
Uniform Trade Secret Act (US)
    109–10
United Kingdom
    blasphemy laws 138–9
    confidentiality protections
        110–12
    defamation law 37
    duty to disclose in 78–80
    English footballer case 87
    freedom of expression in
        172–3
    High Court rulings 23
    House of Lords 38, 78, 93, 108
    Ministry of Defence case 121
    privacy rights and protections
        93–5, 108
    protection for sources 117
    Scotland 87, 137

terrorism laws 179
Welsh footballer case 77
United Nations, *see also* Universal
    Declaration of Human
    Rights
    High Commissioner 138
    Human Rights Committee 91
    terrorism protocols 181
United States, *see also* First
    Amendment to the US
    Constitution
    astroturfing by US Air Force 71
    Communications Decency Act
        23, 69, 79
    confidentiality protections
        109–10
    data protection laws 97–8
    defamation law 38–40
    duty to disclose in 72–8
    local shield laws 119
    privacy rights and protections
        89–90
    subpoenas against bloggers, etc
        60
    Supreme Court rulings 15, 31,
        132–4
Universal Declaration of Human
    Rights
    Article 2 130
    Article 7 130
    Article 11 48
    Article 12 90
    Article 18 131
    Article 19 131, 169
    freedom of expression in
        170–1
University of Northern Colorado
    21
URLs, licence to use 160–1
USA PATRIOT Act (US) 180
USA Today 6
user-generated content 69–70
Uzbekistan 175

Vahrenwald, Arnold 92
van Oosten, Marcel 137
Vera, Gilberto Martinez 182
Victorian Government Solicitor's
  Office 58
Video Privacy Protection Act (US)
  98
Vietnam xiv–xv, 42, 121, 175
Virgin Mobile 1–3
Virginia District Court 171

Wales, *see* United Kingdom
Wardlaw, Kim McClane 140
Warman, Richard 80, 134–5
Warren, Samuel D. 89
Washington Post 52, 64, 122, 126
whistleblowers, immunity for
  120–3, *see also* confidential
  sources
White, William 6, 132–3
Whitehouse, Mary 138–9
Whitman, James Q. 86
WikiLeaks case xvii, 75–6, 122,
  171
Wikimedia 79, 95
Wilders, Geert 137
William, Prince (Duke of
  Cambridge) 94
Williams, Tracy 23
Wilson, Frank Russell 59
WIPO, *see* World Intellectual
  Property Organisation
Wired magazine 99, 157
witnesses 116

Wolf, Josh 118, 171
WordPress 17, 73, 161
World Intellectual Property
  Organisation
  Arbitration and Mediation
    Center 161
  examples of free use 152–3
  list of media types 148–50
  on licensing 155
World Legal Information Institute
  188
World Press Freedom Index
  172–3
writs, service of 61–2
WTForever21 blog 145–7
www.bahamascitizen.com website
  73
www.rosepeaks.com blog 60–1

Xie Jin 41

Yahoo! Holdings 7, 136
Yale Law Journal 86
Yiannopoulos, Milo 12–13
Youth for Climate Truth 73
YouTube 7, 181

Zeta-Jones, Catherine 93, 108
Zimbabwe 176
*Zippo Manufacturing Company v
  Zippo Dot Com, Inc* (US)
  3–4
Zomba Recording 154